# Charles Dickens's England

# Charles Dickens's England

Written by
David Nicholas Wilkinson & Emlyn Price

Photographs by
Russell Burden

Dickens Consultant
Dr Tony Williams
The International Dickens Fellowship

CHARLES DICKENS'S ENGLAND
Written by David Nicholas Wilkinson & Emlyn Price
Photographs by Russell Burden

First published 2009
guerilla books limited
www.guerilla-books.com

Cover Design and book layout by Nebulo Strata.
Printed in China by C&C Offset Printing Co., Ltd.

A catalogue of this book is available from the British Library.

ISBN 13   978-0-9554943-3-8

*This book is dedicated to the men and women of The International Dickens Fellowship, past, present and future.*

*Derek Jacobi researching in Peter Ellis Bookshop, Cecil Court, London, WC2*

*Table of Contents*

# Foreword

Over the many thousands of years during which man has been recording narratives to recount to others, there is just a mere handful of unique story-tellers. Charles Dickens is most assuredly one of these: even those who've never read a word of his works know his tales and characters, through film or television or radio.

Dickens was simply a master. He was also an almost unrivalled genius at creating characters: memorable characters who live, not just on the page but in the mind, long after the reader has closed the book; characters who are also responsible for some of the most profound, funny, astute, pitiable or consequential observations in English literature; characters conjuring up phrases that have long been assimilated into common usage.

For a reader, this is a joy; for an actor, it's a gift. I am extremely fortunate to have played two of his characters, though I would have liked to have played many more: Little Nell's hopeless and incompetent grandfather in *The Old Curiosity Shop* and Arthur Clennam in *Little Dorrit*. The director of the latter, Christine Edzard, was so in awe of the text that she made sure that all the costumes were made exactly as they were in Dickens's day, with everything handmade and sewn. Then, in the evening, all the garments were cleaned by hand. No modern washing machines or dry cleaning for my costume! Thus, she ensured that due consideration would be given to the spirit of this brilliant book and its author.

I was attracted to CHARLES DICKENS'S ENGLAND partly because it was a new challenge for me as I had not presented a documentary before; but ultimately, it was the subject matter. Of course, I know Dickens's work and the worlds he created; but I was struck by just how many of the towns, buildings, churches, public houses, inns and other places that appear in his fiction are based upon actual sites.

Having been born and raised in London, admittedly on the very fringes of the East End, in taking part in this production, I was astonished to discover that the city still boasts baths once used by the Romans, now all but hidden behind a nondescript building in an out of the way side street, or that I could dine in an old fashioned *chop house* where the menu and surroundings are those Dickens would have recognised over one hundred and fifty years ago. How shocking it was to find that Dotheboys Hall was actually a real school, though under a different name: it still exists, transformed today into seven attractive houses. I even got to sleep in not one but two rooms where the great man once laid his head. Extraordinary.

Given Dickens's fame and special place in modern Britain, it was something of a revelation to find that many of his former homes are not adorned with blue plaques announcing this fact, leaving some of their current inhabitants blissfully unaware of their direct link with Bill Sikes or Smike or Sam Weller.

So often when one thinks of Dickens, one instinctively thinks of London. I was therefore fascinated to find out what an enormous influence the county of Kent had on so many of his stories – *Great Expectations, David Copperfield, The Mystery of Edwin Drood, The Pickwick Papers* all draw upon the memories of his idyllic childhood, roaming the fields, lanes and estuaries of the *Garden of England*.

There have been hundreds of books written about Charles Dickens and his life and works, but I am surprised that this is the first coffee-table book which actually offers a contemporary examination of the places in which he lived or those he used to such peerless effect in his stories.

In introducing you to these places in this book and accompanying TV series and DVD which I was privileged to experience so intimately for myself, I really hope that, one day, you too will find an opportunity to see them firsthand for yourselves. It really has been an absolute joy and a revelation.

Derek Jacobi
London 2009

# Introduction

In 1993, I produced and co-wrote a film of the best-selling book, *James Herriot's Yorkshire*. Alf Wight (James Herriot) was extremely ill at the time but had graciously and bravely agreed to appear, saying *'I have given you my word that I would be in the film, therefore I will be in the film.'* After the filming of his interview, on the drive back to his home, he asked me if I planned to make similar films about writers and I said possibly one about Dickens, not having even thought about it before then. He said he would love to see it since Dickens was a hero of his and he would like to see the places Dickens wrote about.

So began my research about Charles Dickens's England. The more I looked into the subject, the more daunted I became, simply because of the vast amount of material it encompassed. The main source books for this project became John Forster's three-volume *The Life of Charles Dickens* and Walter Dexter's excellent trilogy of books, *The London of Dickens, The Kent of Dickens* and *The England of Dickens*. The very first thing I gleaned from these was that Charles Dickens was a man who seemed to me to have lived at least three lifetimes all at once.

Initially, I wrote a treatment based on all the places he lived in, used for his stories or had visited to some effect; and it soon became apparent that, if I were to incorporate absolutely everything, it could be nothing less than several hours long. Then, after re-structuring the concept as a one-off film that could also be edited as a TV series of two forty eight minute episodes, I successfully secured both private finance and a very strong commitment from SkyARTS as co-producers. Therefore our 'tour' was somewhat more restricted by the time allotted to tell the story of his England. It is also important to remember that Dickens was a great creative artist and that not every place or person he wrote about can or should attempt to be related to a real-life original. *Charles Dickens's England* is as much a place of the imagination, or 'fancy' as he would have called it, as it is topographically real.

The distinguished playwright and Oscar winning screenwriter, Ronald Harwood, states that the most important task in adapting a novel into a film is deciding what to take out. So it proved to be for us in constructing a script about the places closely associated with Dickens's life and works. We have, of course, had to leave some elements out; but not all due to time limitations. In researching locations for *Hard Times*, for example, it was almost impossible to find any significant settings that still exist.

Dickens loved to travel and was probably one of the first writers in history to visit so many different locations regularly. Our primary motivation for this publication is to illustrate these places where Dickens lived and about which he wrote; and this we were able to realise through Russell Burden's superb series of original photographs, commissioned exclusively for this book.

If I had any concern in developing this idea, it was the obvious one: how much of Dickens's England still remained? What I did *not* want was a succession of 'this is where such and such used to stand'. Whilst it would have been impossible not to have resorted to this fact of life on occasion, I was pleased to discover how much still remains, even though some places are much altered. The survival is due in large part to the efforts of the men and women of The International Dickens Fellowship who, over many decades, have resisted various developers, councils and modernisers in order to preserve an integral legacy of British Literature. Were it not for them, treasures such as the Charles Dickens Museum in Doughty Street, the Broadstairs Dickens Museum and the Birthplace Museum in Portsmouth would probably not exist as they are today. Indeed, the last of these would have been completely demolished in order to make way for a road widening scheme.

It is for that reason that this book is dedicated to the members of The International Dickens Fellowship past, present and future. Without their efforts, passion and concern for Britain's second greatest writer, our national, historical and literary heritage would be very much the poorer

**David Nicholas Wilkinson**
Producer & Co-Writer

# Portsmouth

When we think of periods in British history, we often refer to them by the reigning monarchs of the time: Georgian, Victorian, Edwardian, Elizabethan. There are also two writers who have achieved the distinction of similar instant recognition, characterising an entire period as their own. One is William Shakespeare, and the other, Charles Dickens.

In 1812, whilst the war against Napoleonic France was reaching its most critical stage, a whole host of men, women and children of all shapes, sizes, classes and backgrounds, came into the world - along with the genius who would create them, Charles John Huffam Dickens.

Charles was born in the city of Portsmouth, home to Britain's premier Royal Navy Port where his father, John Dickens, had been sent to work for the Pay Office. On 7th February 1812, Charles Dickens was born; and though no one was yet aware of it, so was the age we now call 'Dickensian.'

The word itself conjures up a multitude of images - from jolly Christmases around log fires to children suffering in harsh, cruel workhouses; from stagecoach journeys between hospitable inns to a foul-smelling, corpse-ridden Thames. Lurking behind the most delightful character there is always the spectre of a life of misery in a debtors' prison.

The family lived in what was then a Portsmouth suburb at 1 Mile End Terrace, Landport, Portsea - now 393 Old Commercial Road and home of the Dickens Birthplace Museum. An unusually forward-thinking council purchased it for posterity in 1904; but extraordinarily in 1976, a later council tried to demolish it to make way for a road-widening scheme. It was saved by the tireless work of The International Dickens Fellowship whose campaign fortunately persuaded the council of their folly. When the main road was finally diverted and Old Commercial Road closed to through traffic, The International Dickens Fellowship planted a row of saplings to commemorate this near catastrophe.

The Council now cherishes and maintains the Museum for the ever-growing number of visitors who come from all over the world. Sadly, because of the high cost of running such an attraction, the Museum can only open in the summer, much to the disappointment of those whose visits occur at other times. Those who do visit will find that, even today, the Royal Naval fleet can still be glimpsed, as in John Dickens's day, from the windows of the house.

*Opposite page: The Birthplace Museum, Portsmouth*

*Following pages: Artifacts and images at the museum*

# OLD COMMERCIAL ROAD

Charles Dickens Liverland.
Presented to Mrs. Elliot at his Death.
By his Executrix, Miss Hogarth.

| Rent due 25 Mar 1812 | | Rent due 24 June 1812 | |
|---|---|---|---|
| Pearce | 10·10 | Pearce | 10·10 |
| Harding | 4 | Harding | 5·19 |
| Craieze | 13·13 | Craieze | 13·13 |
| Wadge | 1·10·6 | Reevs | 2·17 |
| Reevs | 2·12·6 | Walker | 2·17 |
| Walker | 2·12·6 | Price | 2·17 |
| Price | 2·12·6 | Rachetts | 2·17 |
| Rachett | 2·12·6 | Cox | 2·12·6 |
| Cox | 2·12·6 | Stonson | 2·12·6 |
| Stonson | 2·12·6 | Eyers | 2·17 |
| Eyers | 2·12·6 | Bowyer | 2·17 |
| Bowyer | 2·12·6 | Chiverton | 2·12·6 |
| Chiverton | 2·12·6 | Marshall | 2·12·6 |
| Marshall | 2·12·6 | Bidford | 3·12·9 |
| Bidford | 3·0·3 | Moses | 3·12·9 |
| Moses | 3·0·3 | Darcey | 7·17·6 |
| Darcey | 7·17·6 | Good | 5·5 |
| Good | 5·5 | Dickens | 8·15 |
| Dickens | 8·15 | Smith | 2 |
| Smith | 2 | Harris | 2 |
| Harris | 2 | Clements | 2 |
| Clements | 2 | Kimber | 2·10 |
| Kimber | 2·10 | Hall (Garden) | 2·12·6 |
| Hall (Garden) | 2·12·6 | | |

Charles was the second child of John and Elizabeth Dickens. His father worked as a clerk in the Naval Pay Office in Portsmouth Dockyard. Today, the building is much the same as it was, still accommodating the safe that held the pay for every employee of the Royal Navy at the time. Now, however, it stores important artefacts from the *Mary Rose* ship excavation. On the outside walls of the Pay Office, the marks left by generations of sailors as they queued for their wages can still be seen.

Originally in St. Mary's Church, Portsea, and now to be found in the Copnor Parish Church of St. Alban, stands the 15th Century font used to christen the infant Charles Dickens. Extraordinarily, this was also used to christen one of the other giants of the Victorian age, the revolutionary engineer Isambard Kingdom Brunel, born nearby some six years earlier.

Ironically for someone who worked in a Pay Office with a good salary, financial difficulties were to become increasingly characteristic for John Dickens, leading his family to move to a less costly property at first, until Elizabeth put her foot down and they moved somewhat up-market once again. Neither of these houses, at 16 Hawke Street and 39 Wish Street, Southsea, has survived.

*Left top: The Naval Pay Office where John Dickens*
*worked. This is still part of the Royal Navy's working*
*yard and is therefore restricted to the visitors of*
*The Portsmouth Historic Dockyard*
*Bottom: The safe used by John Dickens*

*Opposite page top: Interior of the old Pay Office*
*Bottom: Marks left by generations of sailors*

*Next spread: 15th Century Font, now in Copnor*
*Parish Church with Rev. Roger Calder*

# London (Infancy)

With the defeat of Napoleon and an end to hostilities, and no longer needed at Portsmouth Dockyard, John Dickens was posted to Somerset House, London, then the Royal Navy's Administrative Headquarters in 1815.

Aged only three, Charles and his family moved to 10 Norfolk Street - now 22 Cleveland Street, London W1. This area, which once accommodated modest working families very much on the fringes of basic survival, today finds itself a vibrant part of London's West End. Not far from the Post Office Tower, it is now largely commercial in nature rather than residential, with few families living locally.

Just two doors away from Charles's former home are the headquarters of Dennis Publishing one of the world's most successful private publishing houses. Founder, owner and poet Felix Dennis is a great admirer of Charles Dickens.

*Right and opposite page: 22 Cleveland Street formally 10 Norfolk Street*

# Chatham

After two years, John Dickens was moved once again, this time to the Pay Office in Chatham, Kent where, after a brief stay at lodgings in High Street, Blue Town, Sheerness, a few miles to the north, the family settled into 2 Ordnance Terrace - now number 11.

As well as being taught to read at an early age by his mother, his imagination was further fuelled by stories from Mary Weller, a family servant, who told him bedtime stories in dramatic fashion, giving the young boy the taste for the theatrical. Another imaginative stimulus came from his father's small collection of 18th-century novels, ranging from *Don Quixote* to the *Arabian Nights*, leading to a lifelong enthusiasm, especially for the latter.

The Pay Office in Chatham Dockyard where John Dickens took up his new post has also changed little in the intervening two centuries. Young Charles would often have played on the steps outside whilst waiting for his father to finish work.

Chatham of the day was, like Portsmouth, a powerhouse for the navy. Charles would have observed the constant bustle of ships and sailors coming and going from all over the world, and women of a certain sort as well, a pot-pourri of activity for his young imagination to start germinating.

*Opposite page: Marion Goktas and Toni Mackintosh, residents of Dickens's childhood home when we filmed*

*Below: Having played in a hayfield opposite his house, an older Dickens later reported that the 'ugly dark monster of a tunnel' of Chatham Railway Station 'had swallowed up the playing field'*

Above: Naval Pay Office

Opposite page: Officers Terrace, Chatham Historic Dockyard

'There are some small out-of-the-way landing places on the Thames and the Medway, where I do much of my summer idling. Running water is favourable to day-dreams, and a strong tidal river is the best of running water for mine. I like to watch the great ships standing out to sea or coming home richly laden, the active little steam-tugs confidently puffing with them to and from the sea-horizon, the fleet of barges that seem to have plucked their brown and russet sails from the ripe trees in the landscape, the heavy old colliers, light in ballast, floundering down before the tide, the light screw barks and schooners imperiously holding a straight course while the others patiently tack and go about, the yachts with their tiny hulls and great white sheets of canvas, the little sailing-boats bobbing to and fro on their errands of pleasure or business, and-- as it is the nature of little people to do--making a prodigious fuss about their small affairs'.
- *from The Uncommercial Traveller*

27

Dickens loved to walk all over the fields, villages, towns and coastline of North Kent with his father, on whose character Mr Micawber is largely based. On one such walk, Gad's Hill Place at Higham was pointed out and he was told *'if he worked very hard he might one day own such a place'*. It would seem that both this comment and the house itself were to have an important effect on Charles later on in his life.

# Rochester

Immediately next to Chatham is Rochester. These towns are inextricably linked and are often referred to as the Medway Towns. Both were to leave a lasting impression upon both Charles's life and his work.

Although not his actual birthplace, the Medway towns were, as his friend and, later, official biographer, John Forster, says, *'the birthplace of his fancy'*; and his thoughts always returned here in his writings.

Charles's joy in learning was nurtured in a school run by William Giles, who recognised the little boy's abilities and gave him great encouragement. Indeed, years later, he marked the success of *The Pickwick Papers* by sending Dickens a silver snuff-box engraved *'to the inimitable Boz.'* Occasionally during this period, encouraged by his father, the young Dickens was asked to sing at the Mitre Tavern in Chatham High Street. This was the happiest time of Dickens's childhood.

Rochester figures under its own name in *The Pickwick Papers*, *David Copperfield* and the *Christmas Stories*. In *Great Expectations*, it is referred to as *'Up town'* and *'Our town'*, and in *Edwin Drood,* it's called Cloisterham. Although he often refers to the city under fictitious names, there is no hiding the fact that he dearly loved Rochester. Writers and historians often talk of Dickens's London, which did undoubtedly have an enormous impact on him. Of equal importance, and some might argue of even greater significance, were the impressions infused within him here in the county of Kent.

*Above: The Old Corn Exchange, Rochester*

*Opposite and next spreads:*
*Rochester Cathedral*

This spread: Dickens is believed to have 'borrowed' some of the names of his characters from headstones in local graveyards. For example, in Rochester Cathedral's graveyard, there is a memorial to the Dorrett Family, which may have served as an inspiration for his novel, Little Dorrit. Although the spelling is not quite the same, the pronunciation certainly is

The cathedral itself also featured in his earlier novel, The Pickwick Papers, and would be used again as a setting in The Mystery of Edwin Drood

# London (Childhood)

At the age of ten, Dickens's idyllic childhood came to an abrupt end when his father was once again posted back to London. Although Charles was permitted to remain at William Giles's school for a few further months after the family left for London in June 1822, he eventually joined them after a most unpleasant coach trip. He describes the damp straw in the coach into which he was *'packed - like game - and forwarded, carriage paid, to the Cross Keys, Wood Street, Cheapside, London.'*

This was once the site of the Cross Keys Inn. Heavily bombed during the war, all that now remains from Dickens's time is a solitary church tower, one of three church's in Wood Street in Dickens's time.

So many of Dickens's stories were rooted in his childhood observations and experiences. In *Great Expectations*, Pip would also endure a five-hour coach journey, arriving in London at precisely this location. It's interesting to note that the light, cheerful stories he was to conjure up tend to reflect the idyll of his countryside childhood, whilst his dark, grave tales are more often set within the unforgiving heart of city life. The young Charles was about to discover this in what was to become a very bleak and difficult period for him.

*Right and opposite page: There were three churches in Wood Street in Dickens's time; however due to the London Blitz and commercial expansion all that remains is one solitary tower*

16 Bayham Street in Camden which would become the young Charles next home no longer exists. Now, this area attracts affluent professionals and is considered to be almost at the city centre. In 1822, however, for the 10 year old Charles Dickens, it was both filthy and on the very fringes of the city.

Just a quarter of a mile up the road was the Middlesex countryside: the river Fleet still flowed above ground nearby; the area of London known as Chalk Farm, less than a mile away, was in Dickens's time a real farm; Kentish Town was a place of country cottages and market gardens that fed London. Dickens was later to describe Bayham Street itself as a *'mean, small tenement with a wretched little back garden abutting on a squalid court.'*

By 1822, John and Elizabeth Dickens had seven children, two of whom died in infancy; the eighth, Augustus, was born in 1827. Their house at Bayham Street was thought to have been the inspiration for Bob Cratchit's house in *A Christmas Carol*. Today, the site of 16 Bayham Street is occupied by The Greenland Road Children's Centre which, given the enormous amount of charitable work the adult Dickens was to undertake, is something he would have heartily approved of, taking the place of the house he was so glad to leave.

With such a large, dependent family, John Dickens was finding it difficult to make ends meet on his paymaster's salary. Two days after his twelfth birthday, young Charles began work at Warren's Blacking Factory, a ramshackle old building which then overlooked the Thames. *'The last house on the left hand-side of the way, at old Hungerford Stairs'* was how he would later describe it. Employment at Warren's had been found for him by a relative, James Lamert.

Hungerford Stairs and the whole Hungerford Market area were demolished in 1860 in preparation for the construction of Charing Cross Railway Station. Long before that, Warren's had moved its premises to Chandos Street, Covent Garden. As for Charles's treasured education during this time, it simply ceased - a fact he would resent for the rest of his life.

Dickens himself described his new life at Warren's, *'My work was to cover the pots of paste-blacking: first with a piece of oil paper, and then with a piece of blue paper, to tie them round with a string; and then to clip the paper close and neat all round, until it looked as smart as a pot of ointment from an apothecary's shop.'* He worked from 8am to 8pm, Monday to Saturday, at 6 shillings per week, and in full public view.

One of the boys Dickens worked alongside was Bob Fagin, a name he would later use to great effect. In *Great Expectations*, the first thing that Joe Gargery does when he comes up to London is to go and look at the *'Blacking Ware'us.'* Although Charles later drew upon these experiences for his stories, he rarely admitted to anyone about his ignominy in having actually worked in such a place. He wrote *'No words can express the secret agony of my soul as I sunk into this companionship, compared these every day associates with those of my happier childhood, and felt my early hopes of growing up to be a learned and distinguished man, crushed in my breast.'*

*Opposite page:*
*Top left: Bayham Street*
*just after Dickens's time*
*Underneath: The site today*
*Bottom Left: The site of*
*Warren's Blacking Factory*
*Top right: Looking down*
*towards where the Blacking*
*Factory used to stand*
*Bottom right: Warren's*
*Blacking Factory*

To add to his woes, a fortnight after Charles started work at Warren's, in 1824, John Dickens entered The Marshalsea Prison for a debt of £40 and 10 shillings.

Between 1329 and 1842, The Marshalsea Prison housed smugglers, mutineers and, most of all, debtors. All that remains of this notorious institution is a solitary wall and there is also an original grille at the Charles Dickens Museum in Doughty Street. Soon after, apart from Charles and his sister, Fanny, the other members of the family joined him there as a more economical means of living, a not unusual practice at the time.

This was a time when a man could be imprisoned for debt and would not be released until his debt was paid in full. In order to earn money to pay the debt, he would have to work, but being in prison made that impossible. This ludicrous situation meant that, without outside assistance, a family might be condemned to a permanent incarceration.

Prisons dominate Dickens's stories: Fagin in the condemned cell; Mr Micawber and William Dorrit, whose circumstances mirror those of John Dickens; and Arthur Clennam who makes no friends in The Marshalsea because he is *'too depressed to associate with the herd in the yard'*. In the preface of *Little Dorrit*, Dickens states that whoever visits this site *'will stand among the crowding ghosts of many miserable years.'*

There was only one person available to break this cycle of debt, and that was Charles. For the first time in his life, in order to bring in an income, he took lodgings with a family friend, Mrs Roylance, at 37 Little College Street, Camden - now College Place. Separated from his family at The Marshalsea, however, as well as working long hours at Warren's in Charing Cross, made this brief stay in Camden far too difficult for the young boy to bear; and so lodgings were found for him in 1 Lant Street, Southwark, so that, at the beginning and end of his working day, he could spend time with his family in the prison.

*Top left: 25, Fitzroy Street*
*Bottom left: The Polygon site*
*Middle: All that remains of Gower*
*Street North*
*Right: 18 Bentinck Street*

*Opposite page:*
*Top: The last remaining Adelphi Arch*
*Middle and bottom: A viaduct arch*
*under Charing Cross Station. It was the*
*construction of the railway terminus that*
*caused the Warren's site to be demolished*

In *The Pickwick Papers*, Charles later recalled, *'There is a repose about Lant Street. The majority of the inhabitants either direct their energies to the letting of furnished apartments or devote themselves to the healthful and invigorating pursuit of mangling.'* But of his lodgings themselves, he said, *'the little window had a pleasant prospect of a timber-yard; and when I took possession of my new abode, I thought it was paradise.'*

After fourteen weeks, John finally inherited enough money in a legacy from his mother to discharge his debts and leave The Marshalsea Prison, but despite successfully negotiating a 'shabby genteel' retirement pension of £145 a year, financial uncertainties still unleashed an unending succession of re-locations upon the Dickens family.

By 1824, the family had already experienced just such a move prior to John's imprisonment to Gower Street North. Although the house is no longer there, the road has become the entrance to the A&E department of University College Hospital. After John's subsequent release from the The Marshalsea, the family settled in 29 Johnson Street, Somers Town - now Cranleigh Street - until 1827 when they were evicted for non-payment. They then moved around the corner to The Polygon, Clarendon Square, Somers Town, followed in 1829 by a return to Norfolk Street once again. Then came 15 Fitzroy Street - now number 25 and very much changed since Dickens's day, followed in 1833 to 18 Bentinck Street - now rebuilt!

This was the time when the young Dickens began
to find his feet in London. Most days, while working
at Warren's factory, he would have passed the
Adelphi Arches. Built by the Adam brothers and
completed during the 1770s, the Adelphi Arches
comprised twenty-four terraced houses by the
riverside. However, between 1864-70, the Victoria
Embankment was constructed, depriving it of its
desirable riverside situation. Eventually, by 1938,
Royal Terrace was demolished. Today, only one
solitary arch remains.

Dickens would later use the arches in *David
Copperfield* who recounts: '*I was fond of wandering
about the Adelphi because it was a mysterious place,
with those dark arches.*'

And in *Little Dorrit*, he describes it as a place
where '*there is a sudden pause... to the roar of the great
thoroughfare. The many sounds become so deadened that
the change is like putting cotton on the ears, or having
the head thickly muffled.*'

It was while Dickens was working at Warren's Blacking Factory that it moved just across the Strand to Chandos Street, Covent Garden. Soon after this relocation, John quarrelled with James Lamert who ran the factory and Charles was sacked. But his mother interceded, in an attempt to re-secure his post, to Charles's eternal resentment: *'I never afterwards forgot, I never shall forget, I never can forget, that my mother was warm for my being sent back.'*

Fortunately for Charles, something prompted his father to insist he resume his education and he went to Wellington House Academy located on the corner of Hampstead Road and Granby Street. This rescued him from a life of manual drudgery and pointed him in a direction where his brain would take precedence over his brawn. His time at the Blacking Factory was over at last.

In 1827, once again, his father's debts predictably forced Charles to withdraw from school; and aged fifteen, his formal education came to an end. He later matter-of-factly described leaving school as *'tolerably early, for my father was not a rich man and I had to begin the world.'*

It was during this time, that Charles began the process of self-education that was to inform his entire professional life. At the earliest possible opportunity, on his eighteenth birthday, he obtained a reader's ticket to the British Museum, educating himself in its Reading Room.

*Top right: The site of Warren's Blacking Factory when it moved to Chandos Street*
*Bottom right: Wellington House Academy*
*Opposite: The British Museum, London*

Dickens was also now at liberty to socialise. He was always pleased to visit his uncle Thomas Barrow, who lived in the upper house of a bookseller, at 10 Gerrard Street. Although the bookseller himself, Mr. Manson, had died in 1812, his widow had carried on the business. One of the innumerable treasures she lent to the curious young Dickens was George Colman's *Broad Grins*, which included descriptions of London life and characters. Charles was particularly taken by a description of Covent Garden, which he then visited to compare it with the book. He later described it as *'snuffing up the flavour of the faded cabbage-leaves as if it were the very breath of comic fiction.'* Years later, Mr Jaggers of *Great Expectations* would also reside in Gerrard Street, possibly in the very same house.

In 1827, Charles entered the adult world of employment as a junior clerk in the office of Ellis & Blackmore, solicitors. The drudgery of this work prompted the ambitious Charles to teach himself shorthand, the Gurney system, in order to pursue journalism. He would later describe Gurney's shorthand in *David Copperfield* as *'that savage stenographic mystery.'* In eighteen months, he mastered a system that took others three years to learn. This was thought of as the equivalent of learning six languages. The phonetics of this shorthand also helped train his ear for the idiosyncrasies of speech amongst the characters he was to create.

*Above: Another enticement at this time lay at Prince Henry's Room, Fleet Street. Built in 1610, it is one of the few inns to survive the fire of London and later became 'Mrs. Salmon's Waxworks', a favourite visit for the young Dickens. David Copperfield would also take Peggotty here 'to see some waxworks in Fleet Street'*

*Opposite page top left:*
*10 Gerrard Street*
*Other images: Today Gerrard Street is London's China Town*

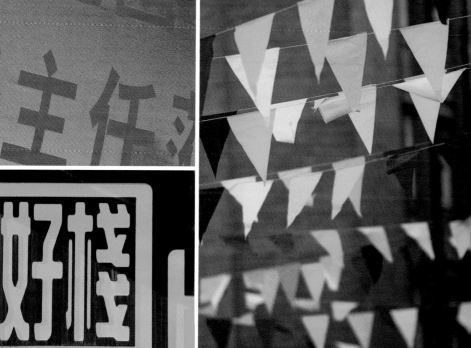

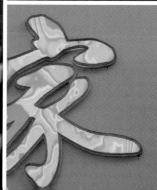

*Above: St Paul's Cathedral*

*Opposite page: Houses of Parliament and Lord Hattersley*

In late 1828, Charles at last became a newspaper reporter, near St. Paul's Cathedral, at Doctors' Commons, hearing cases dealing with ecclesiastical, admiralty, probate and divorce matters. Although Doctors' Commons was abolished years later, it served to provide experience whilst waiting for a vacancy to arise at the House of Commons for Dickens to become a Parliamentary reporter.

By early 1832, Charles had joined the parliamentary staff reporting, John Barrow's periodical, *The Mirror of Parliament*. This work was well paid but utterly exhausting. Nevertheless, his rise was rapid due to his speedy, accurate reporting under dreadful conditions. At the same time, he also worked as a general reporter on the radical, *True Sun*. He excelled at such journalism because he could write at lightning speed, as he would continue to do throughout his professional life.

During his time as a Parliamentary reporter, Dickens saw two great instruments going through: The Great Reform Bill of 1832, which made things more democratic; and The Poor Law Reform Act of 1834 which was the most brutal act to go through parliament in the nineteenth century. It made poverty a crime. It was intended to punish the paupers - not by giving them outlaw status, but by sending them into work houses. It was the beginning of the great Workhouse Movement - Workhouses were intended to be brutal and unpleasant because the paupers were responsible for their own poverty and ought to be punished. And therefore, if you were destitute in the parish, your family was broken up - women in one with their children, men in another - required to work, living on minimum levels of subsistence and being actually identified as being responsible for this drain on society.

     The workhouse was just supposed to offer subsistence. But it also wanted to make poverty a penalty. It held the view that the poor were, in some way, criminally responsible for their poverty; so they were to be humiliated, they were to be punished. They were to be forced to work, and they were to be forced to live on the minimum standards.

     When Dickens was twice approached to stand as an MP, he described the House of Commons as 'pompous'. And I think, his reaction was because of the rather low quality of the members of parliament. It was not quite a job for people of ability and talent; it was a gentleman's spare-time occupation.

     In dealing with social problems, such as By-Election corruption, Dickens was more effective than other writers because he wrote about great issues in a humorous way, and that made it intellectually more accessible, much more digestible. And therefore people laugh at first; but when they've had a day to think about it, think 'there's something wrong with that' as well, on another level.

     There was also a passion with Dickens. I think he really believed in the need to reform. Others recognised it in an intellectual sort of way; but, I suspect, Dickens felt something in his heart about the way it's wrong the way the poor are treated, the way the vast majority are treated.

     He drew attention to their plight. I think he did more about it than people in parliament. People in there were doing very little about it until 1906, until the first great reforming radical Liberal government. The people in the House of Commons didn't think that the welfare of the poor was their responsibility. That was someone else's responsibility; or perhaps no one's responsibility. Parliament didn't have anything to do with poverty and welfare.

ROY HATTERSLEY
*Former Member of Parliament and now a Member of the House of Lords*

By 1830, his love-life had developed with his first serious sweetheart, Maria Beadnell, often claimed to be the source of Dora in *David Copperfield*. Her father managed the banking house of Smith, Payne & Smith at 1 Lombard Street - now a restaurant. Maria was something of a flirt and the relationship ended after a stormy courtship of three years in a painful rejection which deeply affected Dickens thereafter, vowing never to leave himself open to such vulnerability again. Nevertheless, he wrote of her *'I have never loved and I can never love any human creature breathing but yourself'*, and he may have been right. In later life however, after a very brief and surprising re-acquaintance, she became his inspiration for Flora Finching in *Little Dorrit*.

During this emotionally unsettling time, Charles, aged twenty, even applied to the stage manager at Covent Garden Theatre to audition as an actor but, fortunately for literature, he was too ill to attend the appointment. This was also the time when the young Dickens began to hone his observations of the curiosities that populated the capital's streets. He visited the theatres regularly, as well as perfecting his 'mimicry' to the great amusement of his colleagues. This ambition to be involved in the theatre would never leave him. There is a story, possibly apocryphal, that a stagehand said to Dickens years later, when he was presenting his public readings, *'Oh Mr Dickens, what a loss it was to the stage when you took to writing books.'*

Johnson's Court, named after Dr. Johnson who compiled the first English dictionary, runs off Fleet Street, then London's newspaper and magazine district. Sweeney Todd, the Demon Barber had a shop just around the corner. In 1833, the offices of *The Monthly Magazine* were located there. Charles Dickens later recounted that he *'dropped stealthily one evening at twilight, with fear and trembling, into a dark letter-box, in a dark office, up a dark court in Fleet Street'* the anonymous short story manuscript of *A Sunday Out Of Town*. Although the court is still there, sadly the building is not.

Two months later Dickens would walk nervously into a bookshop in the nearby Strand to pick up a first edition of the magazine hot off the press. As he flicked through the pages, he discovered *'in all the glory of print'* that his story had in fact been published under the title of *A Dinner At Poplar Walk*. The owner of the magazine, Captain Holland, could not afford to pay any of the contributors, but he was so impressed with the young Dickens that he asked him for more 'sketches' which he duly published. Although the first story was un-credited, all subsequent stories appeared under the name of 'Boz.' Dickens borrowed the name from his brother, Augustus, who pronounced his own nickname, Moses, as 'Boses' when young. The family shortened this to Boz. So, although he did not receive any financial recompense, he received the full artistic credit.

*Opposite page:*
*Left: Maria Beadnell*
*Right: 1 Lombard Street*
*Bottom: Royal Opera House, Covent Garden*

*Above: Dr Johnson's House*

*Mr. Augustus Minns was a bachelor, of about forty as he said - of about eight-and-forty as his friends said. He was always exceedingly clean, precise, and tidy; perhaps somewhat priggish, and the most retiring man in the world. He usually wore a brown frock-coat without a wrinkle, light inexplicables without a spot, a neat neckerchief with a remarkably neat tie, and boots without a fault; moreover, he always carried a brown silk umbrella with an ivory handle. He was a clerk in Somerset-house, or, as he said himself, he held 'a responsible situation under Government.'*

**The opening chapter of** **A Dinner At Poplar Walk**

( later published as Mr Minns and his Cousin)

Below: Somerset House, Dickens's father also worked.

Opposite Page:

Top: the site of Furnivals Inn

Middle right: Catherine Dickens

Bottom: 11, Selwood Terrace, Chelsea

By this time, as well as joining the *Morning Chronicle,* the chief rival to *The Times,* Charles had also written twelve 'sketches' for *Bell's Life in London* and, more importantly, twenty 'street sketches' for the *Evening Chronicle,* edited by George Hogarth, the man who was to become his future father-in-law.

In 1834, aged twenty-two, Charles left his father's house in Bentinck Street with the intention of starting a home of his own. After a brief stay in bachelor rooms, first in Cecil Street off the Strand and then in Buckingham Street – neither building survives today - he rented chambers at 13 Furnival's Inn in Holborn. Furnival's Inn was pulled down and replaced with the rather splendid red-brick Victorian gothic revival building which, for a great many years, was the headquarters of a major insurance company, Prudential Assurance. In its courtyard, there is a bust of Charles Dickens on prominent display for public viewing, sculptured by Percy Fitzgerald who was himself a member of Dickens's circle of friends.

A mere three months after meeting George Hogarth's daughter, Catherine, who was physically not unlike Maria Beadnell but lacked her coquettish nature, Charles and Catherine were engaged. So smitten was he that he took on additional lodgings at 11 Selwood Terrace in Brompton, West London in order to be closer to her.

During this period, Dickens began to move in a more noteworthy social circle of friends and acquaintances. He was befriended by Harrison Ainsworth, a popular novelist of the time. He was also introduced to Benjamin Disraeli, Edward Bulwer-Lytton, Daniel Maclise, George Cruikshank and the publisher, John Macrone, who suggested publishing two volumes of 'sketches', with illustrations by Cruikshank. *Sketches by Boz* was published in 1836, earning Dickens £150 and attracting one commission after another. Charles was making a name for himself at last; and it wasn't long before work started on the instalments that would make up his first novel, *The Posthumous Papers of the Pickwick Club* or *The Pickwick Papers.*

# The Pickwick Papers

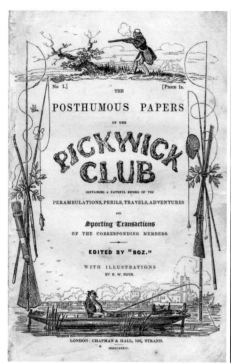

The association between Robert Seymour and Charles Dickens bore all the ingredients for an archetypal clash of artistic temperaments. Seymour was an artist concealing an inclination towards an overwhelming hypersensitivity; while Dickens was a literary phenomenon on the threshold of self-discovery and belief.

Seymour envisaged an idea for a series of sporting sketches, and his publishers, Chapman & Hall, approached Dickens to provide the text. Fired with enthusiasm, Dickens soon insisted upon choosing the themes. After misunderstandings that were likely to have arisen from their separate talks with the publishers, as they began work, each was convinced he was in charge of the direction it would take; and although they had not yet physically met, frictions arose almost immediately, a situation that never improved.

After an increasing frustration with each other's contributions which would have greatly added to Seymour's growing state of anxiety, dissatisfied with the illustrations for the 2nd instalment, Dickens told Seymour that he must do as he was told. Feeling utterly humiliated by what he perceived as a reversal in his standing in a project that had originally sprung from him, Seymour dutifully re-engraved the plates, accidentally spoiling one. After agonisingly re-doing the spoiled plate, the following morning, he went outside behind his garden studio and shot himself in a moment later officially described as 'temporary insanity'.

Amongst those interviewed by Dickens to replace Seymour were Robert William Buss, William Makepeace Thackeray and Hablôt Knight Browne. Later, both Buss and Thackeray confidently believed themselves appointed. Indeed, Buss turned down all other offers of work, while Thackeray celebrated by treating himself and Browne to sausages and mash. In the event, Browne was ultimately chosen and went on to illustrate many of Dickens's future works under the pseudonym 'Phiz'.

**ADRIAN WOOTTON**
**Chief Executive, Film London and Dickens enthusiast**

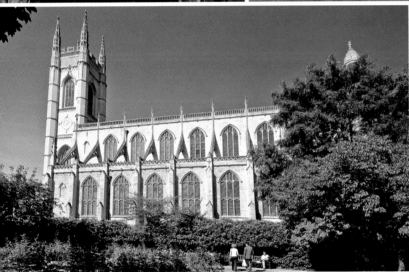

On 2nd April 1836, Charles, aged twenty-four, and Catherine, aged twenty, married in St. Lukes Church, Chelsea. Their first home together as a married couple involved a move to somewhat larger rooms at number 15 Furnival's Inn where they were joined by Catherine's younger sister, Mary, aged sixteen, to whom Dickens was devoted, as well as Frederick, Charles's brother. Dickens was to discover that Catherine simply did not have the temperament to suit the energy of her husband. *'It was as if she had been tied to the tail of a comet.'*

*Above: One mile from Gravesend, on the Rochester Road, stands Craddock's Cottage in Chalk, Kent. It has a plaque claiming it was Charles Dickens's honeymoon cottage; however, others suggest the actual house was over the road and is now demolished. In any event, their fortnight's honeymoon in Chalk turned out to be the only brief time they were alone together throughout their entire married life*

Dickens would also use nearby Gravesend many times over the ensuing years in several of his novels. As well as being a busy port, Gravesend was one of England's earliest seaside resorts. In *Great Expectations*, Pip and his friend, Herbert Pocket, tried to smuggle Magwitch out of the country here. In *Barnaby Rudge*, when Joe Willet enlists in the army, he is transported from London to Gravesend where he then marches off with the rest of the soldiers to Chatham. David Copperfield and Aunt Betsey go to Gravesend to bid 'au revoir' to Mr. Micawber and family when they set off for a new life in Australia. Possibly recalling his own experience just two miles away, in *Bleak House*, Prince Turveydrop and Caddy Jellyby spend their honeymoon in Gravesend.

*Right and Opposite page:*
*Gravesend*

Whilst Dickens stayed in Chalk, he was well advanced in the writing of *The Pickwick Papers*, a story which incorporated more actual recognisable places than any of his later novels. One of these was just a few miles away. Appearing under its real name, The Bull Hotel, Rochester in *The Pickwick Papers*, it would also feature in *Great Expectations* as The Blue Boar. Although it has been greatly modernised inside, the structure today is still very much as it was in Dickens's time. Stage coaches would arrive at the rear, with some passengers alighting from the coach whilst new passengers joined. Then they would set off once again by the front entrance to continue on with their journey.

Further up Rochester High Street, Eastgate House was re-christened Westgate House in *The Pickwick Papers*, also featuring later as the Nuns' House, a school for young ladies, in *The Mystery of Edwin Drood*.

The Leather Bottle in Cobham Kent, is a half-timbered Inn dating from 1629 during the reign of Charles I and named after a leather bottle discovered there in 1720 containing gold sovereigns. As well as featuring in *The Pickwick Papers* when Pickwickians visited *'the clean and commodious village ale house'* in search of Tracy Tupman, Dickens himself also stayed here. Today, it continues to offer food, accommodation and an absolutely priceless charm, as well as a superb collection of memorabilia associated with Dickens.

Dickens stayed there numerous times in room six, which is still available for guest bookings today. Other hotels where the modern Dickens enthusiast can stay in a room once occupied by the great writer include The Angel Bury St Edmunds, the Royal Albion, Broadstairs, York House Hotel - now the Royal Hotel, Bath and Winterbourne House on the Isle of Wight.

*Opposite page: Eastgate House, Rochester*

*This is the actual stone with the rather cryptic inscription which, thinking it a treasure of great antiquity, Mr. Pickwick purchased and took to London.*

*'This is some very old inscription, existing perhaps long before the ancient alms-houses in this place. It must not be lost.'*

*He tapped at the cottage door. A labouring man opened it.*

*'Do you know how this stone came here, my friend?' inquired the benevolent Mr. Pickwick.*

*'No, I don't, Sir,' replied the man civilly. 'It was here long afore I was born, or any on us.'*

*Mr. Pickwick glanced triumphantly at his companion.*

*'You--you--are not particularly attached to it, I dare say,' said Mr. Pickwick, trembling with anxiety. 'You wouldn't mind selling it, now?'*

*'Ah! but who'd buy it?' inquired the man, with an expression of face which he probably meant to be very cunning.*

*'I'll give you ten shillings for it, at once,' said Mr. Pickwick, 'if you would take it up for me.'*

**THELMA GROVE**
**Honorary Life Member, International Dickens Fellowship**

*Opposite page: The Leather Bottle, Cobham, Kent*

61

# Covent Garden

Dickens was to fill his stories with locations easily recognisable to many readers. He was particularly taken with Covent Garden, then London's wholesale fruit, flower and vegetable market, which made an early appearance in *The Pickwick Papers* when Job Trotter spent a night in a vegetable basket there before Pickwick's release, and would subsequently feature in several of his stories. John Forster described his fascination when walking there, *'especially if it were anywhere about Covent Garden or The Strand, perfectly entranced him with pleasure.'*

Steerforth informs David Copperfield that, *'I'm going to breakfast with one of those fellows who is at the Piazza Hotel, Covent Garden'* - an hotel which was actually known as Cuttris's where Dickens himself stayed in 1844 when he returned from Italy. Sadly it is no longer there.

In *Sketches By Boz*, he writes, *'Covent Garden Market, and the avenues leading to it, are thronged with all sorts, sizes, and descriptions, from the heavy lumbering wagon, with its four stout horses, to the jingling costermonger's cart, with its consumptive donkey. The pavement is already strewn with decayed cabbage leaves, broken haybands, and all the indescribable litter of a vegetable market; men are shouting, carts backing, horses neighing, boys fighting, basket women talking, piemen expurgating on the excellence of their pastry, and the donkies braying. These and a hundred other sounds form a compound discordant enough to a Londoner's ears, and remarkably disagreeable to those of country gentlemen who are sleeping at the Hummums for the first time.'* The Hummums was an hotel on the corner of Russell Street.

In *Martin Chuzzlewit*, Ruth and Tom Pinch stroll through the market. In Chapter One of *The Old Curiosity Shop*, Dickens writes, *'Covent Garden at sunrise too, in the spring or summer when the fragrance of sweet flowers is in the air, overpowering even the unwholesome streams of last night's debauchery, and driving the dusky thrush, whose cage is hung outside a garret window all night long, half mad with joy! Poor bird!'.*

In *The Uncommercial Traveller: Night Walks*, Dickens writes, *'Covent Garden Market, when it was market morning, was wonderful company. The great waggons of cabbages, with growers' men and boys lying asleep under them, and with sharp dogs from market-garden neighbourhoods looking after the whole, were as good as a party. But one of the worst night sights I know in London, is to be found in the children who prowl about this place; who sleep in the baskets, fight for the offal, dart at any object they think they can lay their thieving hands on, dive under the carts and barrows, dodge the constables, and are perpetually making a blunt pattering on the pavement of the Piazza with the rain of their naked feet. A painful and unnatural result comes of the comparison one is forced to institute between the growth of corruption as displayed in the so much improved and cared for fruits of the earth, and the growth of corruption as displayed in these all uncared for (except inasmuch as ever-hunted) savages.'*

When the wholesale fruit, flower and vegetable market was moved away from Covent Garden in the 1970s, pulling it all down to make way for a modern office complex had been given serious consideration. Mercifully, good sense prevailed and the area survived relatively unscathed, making it, today, an extremely popular tourist attraction.

On the day we filmed the Covent Garden sequence Russell, the photographer, asked highly talented folk musician Terry St. Clair if he could take his photograph. Terry asked what he was doing and he said it was for a project about Charles Dickens. Terry turned out to be an enthusiastic fan.

*' I love Dickens. I would read one of his London books and set about seeing if I could find the locations he used. Then I would move on to the next book and do the same. I was especially impressed by how effectively he used Covent Garden where I often perform. Dickens was London. He was the Bob Dylan of his day. He was a protest writer. Charles Dickens was a genius who cared for the less fortunate.'*
*TERRY ST. CLAIR*
*Folk Singer*

# The Pickwick Papers
## - continuing the journey

Jack Bamber the legal clerk told Mr. Pickwick many stories of the Inns of Court, especially Clifford's Inn, which cropped up again and again in subsequent Dickens stories such as *Little Dorrit, Our Mutual Friend* and *Bleak House.*

The George & Vulture features prominently in *The Pickwick Papers.* Mr Pickwick and his friends found that it provided *'very good old-fashioned and comfortable quarters'* when they stayed here when the action for breach of promise was going through, and it was here they were served with subpoenas to appear in court at the Guildhall. The George & Vulture is also thought to be London's oldest existing tavern, dating back to 1746, with an inn having been on that site since 1268.

This splendid, delightfully-preserved city restaurant is surely an essential experience for any Dickens enthusiast. The menu, one feels, is something Dickens would recognise and relish. No tiny portions here, drizzled with balsamic vinegar and finished off with a raspberry jus. Instead, the diner can tuck into hearty fare such as Barnsley Chops, Lamb Hot Pot, Steak and Kidney Pie, Grills, Potted Shrimps; accompanied by potatoes, buttered cabbage and good staple British vegetables, all washed down with Yorkshire ale.

In Dickens's own lifetime, this was a popular place for him to come and bring friends and entertain. Since his time, it has maintained its connection with the Dickens family, right the way through and up to the present time, particularly through the activities of Dickens's great grandson, Cedric Dickens. The involvement of Cedric Dickens was enormously important because The George & Vulture has been under threat of demolition on a number of different occasions all the way through the twentieth century. Certainly when Cedric was able to support it and defend it, he did and it's largely through his efforts that The George & Vulture kept going. Cedric died in 2006; he was in his ninetieth year.

The George & Vulture was one of Dickens's favourite watering holes and he would certainly recognise it if he was with us here today. He would notice a number of things with which he would be very, very familiar. It's changed very little. It does capture a sense of what those places were like to dine in. He did use them frequently, and he used them in the novels as well. Famously, in January 1837, he invited a group of thirty-four people here for supper which cost, with wine, £11/5/0 (Eleven pounds and five shillings – today, approximately £1,000).

It was in The Pickwick Papers that he particularly made use of The George & Vulture. It was where Mr. Pickwick stayed because it was a place with accommodation so that when Mr. Pickwick could no longer stay at his lodgings in Goswell Street with Mrs. Bardell because the breach of promise case was coming on at the Guildhall, not very far from here, he stayed in The George & Vulture. And at one point, one of the other characters, Bob Sawyer, said to him, 'I say old boy, where do you hang out?'; to which Mr. Pickwick replies that he was 'at present suspended at "The George and Vulture".'

**DR TONY WILLIAMS**
**The International Dickens Fellowship**

*Opposite page and following spread: The George & Vulture, London EC3*

The Pickwick Clubs were another interesting spin off from *The Pickwick Papers*. Very soon after the novel was published, there were Pickwick Clubs founded – the idea of them being gatherings of people to celebrate in the way that the characters in the novel celebrate: lots of good food, lots of conviviality, lots of good cheer. Those Pickwick Clubs started in 1837 and carried on right the way through to the present day. Once again, Cedric Dickens was a great supporter of the Pickwick Clubs, all over the world and there are a lot of them. Current members of the Pickwick Club meet in the George & Vulture regularly.

All the members of the Pickwick Club have a sobriquet, a name of one of the characters in *The Pickwick Papers*, so the Secretary of the Pickwick Club is always referred to as 'Augustus Snodgrass', with most of the other members adopting the names of other characters. It is exclusive. A lot of the people who are members of the Pickwick Club are people of considerable importance within the financial world, the City of London - past Lord Mayors, present Lord Mayors and people who will in future become Lord Mayors. It is a high-powered organisation, but an organisation that does a lot of good for charitable purposes.

It all reminds us about the reason behind Dickens writing about food and celebration and meals. If we stay with *The Pickwick Papers*, there are breakfasts after breakfasts, and suppers and dinners and lunches – a constant stream of meals being eaten and vast amounts being drunk. Dickens, himself, was a man of very abstemious tastes; yet we get this sense from his writing about these enormous meals people are consuming. It was the sentiment of the thing rather than the thing itself which was important. That, I think, is a good message to take on about Dickens and entertainment and food and drink generally. It is the feelings that come through that are important. It is the sense of belonging, the sense of celebration, the sense of being with friends, the sense of sharing one another's company. The novels give a very strong sense of the kinds of meals people ate in the nineteenth century.

But we can also get a flavour from Dickens's wife, Catherine, who produced a book of 'bills of fare' for dinner parties, from domestic meals for two to three people right up to large gatherings of eighteen or twenty people. She first published this book called *What Shall We Have For Dinner* in 1851 and then, at various intervals, during the course of the 1850s. She wrote it under a pseudonym, as Lady Maria Clutterbuck, a character she had played in a piece of amateur theatre called *Used Up* in which Dickens had involved her. Dickens wrote the preface to the book. From those menu lists and the recipes, it all helps build a sense of what it was like to dine in the nineteenth century.

At the Spaniards Inn, Hampstead (then The Spaniards Tea Gardens), Mrs. and Master Bardell spent an afternoon with Mrs. Raddle, Mr. Raddle and friends. Tracked down by Mr. Jackson, clerk to Dodson & Fogg, Mrs. Bardell was conveyed to the Fleet Prison for the costs in the Bardell versus Pickwick trial.

Dickens had visited East Anglia in January 1835 to report on election nominations for the *Morning Chronicle* and was familiar with The Angel Hotel, Bury St Edmunds, using it to great effect in *The Pickwick Papers*:

*'The coach rattled through the well paved streets of a handsome little town, of thriving and cleanly appearance, and stopped before a large inn situated in a wide open street, nearly facing the old abbey'.*

*'And this,' said Mr Pickwick, looking up, 'is the Angel...'*

He returned to this area on a reading tour in October 1859, where he read at the Athenaeum, near to The Angel, where he stayed, reporting that he had *'a fine room.'*

Opposite page: The Spaniards Inn,
Hampstead NW3

This page: The Angel Hotel,
Bury St Edmunds, Suffolk

Even at the time of its writing, *The Pickwick Papers* commemorates a bygone age, celebrating the journey by stage coach, albeit from a romantic point of view.

Dickens even borrowed the name of his leading man from a well known stage coach proprietor in Bath, Moses Pickwick. And en route to that city by coach, Sam Weller makes a similar observation.

*As Sam spoke he pointed to that part of the coach door on which the proprietor's name usually appears; and there, sure enough, in gilt letters of a goodly size, was the magic name of PICKWICK! "Dear me," exclaimed Mr. Pickwick, quite staggered by the coincidence; "what a very extraordinary thing!" "Yes, but that ain't all," said Sam, again directing his master's attention to the coach door; "not content vith writin' up Pickwick, they puts 'Moses' afore it, vich I call addin' insult to injury, as the parrot said ven they not only took him from his native land, but made him talk the English langwidge arterwards".*

This inclusion may very possibly be the first example of *product placement* in a fictional story. Moses Pickwick also owned 'The White Hart Hotel' which was later demolished to make way for the Grand Pump Room Hotel. The Pickwickians stayed at 'The White Hart.'

The Pickwick Papers is also an early example of the travel story genre, what filmmakers refer to as *road movies*. Dickens was extremely deft at using the English countryside, towns and villages and the people who lived in them, weaving them all enjoyably into the stories, and none more so than Mr Pickwick's sojourn in Bath.

*Opposite page top: The Roman Baths and The Pump Room in Bath, Somerset*

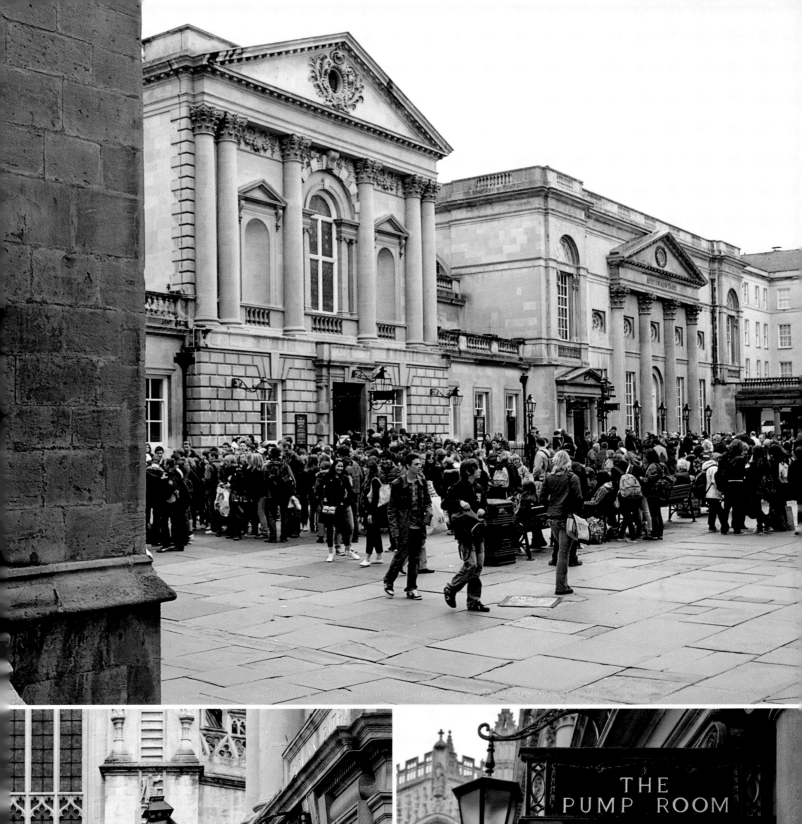

*'As Mr. Pickwick contemplated a stay of at least two months in Bath, he deemed it advisable to take private lodgings for himself and friends for that period; and as a favourable opportunity offered for their securing, on moderate terms, the upper portion of a house in the Royal Crescent, which was larger than they required, Mr. and Mrs. Dowler offered to relieve them of a bedroom and sitting-room.  This proposition was at once accepted, and in three days' time they were all located in their new abode, when Mr. Pickwick began to drink the waters with the utmost assiduity.  Mr. Pickwick took them systematically.  He drank a quarter of a pint before breakfast, and then walked up a hill; and another quarter of a pint after breakfast, and then walked down a hill; and, after every fresh quarter of a pint, Mr. Pickwick declared, in the most solemn and emphatic terms, that he felt a great deal better; whereat his friends were very much delighted, though they had not been previously aware that there was anything the matter with him.'*

At the Assembly Rooms, Bath, Pickwick and his companions would attend Balls. There, all manner of mankind was on display.

*'And lastly, seated on some back benches, where they had already taken up their positions for the evening, were diverse unmarried ladies past their grand climacteric, who not dancing because there were no partners for them, and not play cards lest they should be set down as irretrievably single, were in a favourable situation of being able to abuse everybody without reflection on themselves.'*

*Opposite page: The Royal Crescent, Bath*
*This page: Glass panels above various doors*

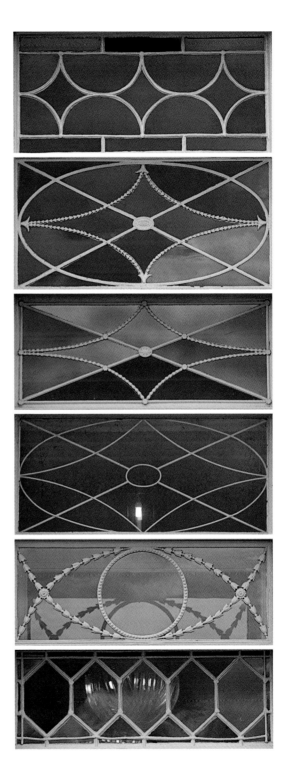

It was also in Bath when staying with his friend, Walter Savage Landor, that Dickens conceived the idea for *Little Nell*, the central character of *The Old Curiosity Shop*. John Forster records that Landor had meant to purchase the house *'and then have it burnt to the ground, to the end that no meaner association should ever desecrate the birthplace of Little Nell.'*

As strange as it may seem today, when *The Pickwick Papers* first appeared in a monthly serial form, earning Dickens £14 per month, it was not initially well received, printing just four hundred copies of the first instalment. Following the issue of the fourth instalment, with the introduction of Sam Weller, all that soon changed, and by the story's end, sales had increased to forty thousand copies.

Later, Dickens was accused of tawdriness for publishing his works in periodicals; but his response to this allegation was that he wished them to be available to all people, not only those who could afford the one and a half guineas demanded for a bound volume - approximately £75 in today's money. Certainly each instalment of his works was eagerly anticipated by all classes of people, much as many today await the next episode of their favourite soap-opera.

*Opposite page: The Assembly Rooms*

*Right: St James's Square*
*The house in which Little Nell was born*

# The Charles Dickens Museum

Such was his newfound status that, by 1837, rather than simply reporting on events for journals, which he would continue to do throughout his life, he was now building up a very successful career in writing fiction and, in the process, developing a reputation that was to make him one of the most popular writers of the age.

In April 1837, Dickens was able to take a three year lease on 48 Doughty Street, London, at a cost of £80 a year (around £4,000 in today's money). Dickens described the house as a *'pleasant twelve-room dwelling of pink brick, with three stories and an attic, a white arched entrance door on the street level, and a small private garden in the rear. It was located just north of Gray's Inn ... a genteel private street with a lodge at each end and gates that were closed at night by a porter in a gold-laced hat and a mulberry-colored coat with the Doughty arms on its buttons.'*

48 Doughty Street became The Dickens House Museum in 1925 and is now known as The Charles Dickens Museum, today holding the world's most important collection of objects associated with the life and works of Charles Dickens; it is also the headquarters of The International Dickens Fellowship, founded in 1902. In that time, a wealth of manuscripts, rare editions, paintings, original furniture and other artefacts, such as the Grille from The Marshalsea Prison, have either been bequeathed by Dickens collectors or else purchased by The Fellowship, with many on permanent display.

Although he only lived in the house for just two years, thanks to the intervention of The Dickens Fellowship who saved it from demolition by purchasing it in 1924, it remains the sole surviving house in London that Dickens enjoyed as an adult family home.

*Above and opposite page: The Charles Dickens Museum, 48 Doughty Street, London WC1*

Most of the house is open to the public with just a few of its rooms occupied by staff for administrative purposes. Over twenty five thousand visitors a year walk in Dickens's footsteps - in The Morning Room, The Dining Room, The Drawing Room, The Study and the Bedrooms, and even down in his Basement.

There are numerous manuscripts on display as well as the increasingly rare monthly or weekly part-works of his stories. On all the walls of each of the rooms are paintings and illustrations either belonging to Dickens himself or relating to his work.

The basement of 49 Doughty Street next door is used by the Museum as a research room and is open to scholars with its impressive collection of books and periodicals from its private library. Some of the research for CHARLES DICKENS'S ENGLAND was undertaken there.

Dickens was very keen on entertaining and, in the Dining Room at Doughty Street, would have had dinner parties with the circle of friends that he was developing - people of literary, theatrical and political importance. This was not the Dickens of iconic image, an old man with a beard. This was a very young man at the early stages of his career, something of a Regency dandy with long, flowing locks and given to brightly-coloured waistcoats, a taste which stayed with him all his life.

A clock from the offices of Moses Pickwick's coaching company is now on display in the Dining Room.

Dickens arrived at 48 Doughty Street with Catherine, his young wife of just a year, and their baby son, Charley, who had lately been born on Twelfth Night. This was initially a very happy time for all who lived there.

There were significant births in the house: two further children, Mary and Kate, heralding the growth of a family which would eventually lead to ten children in all, with one dying in infancy. But there was also one very significant death.

Very close to the young married couple was Catherine's younger sister, Mary, who got on very well with the couple and spent a lot of time with them. And once they'd moved to Doughty Street, Mary was a frequent visitor, very often staying in the house.

On 6th May 1837, about a month after they'd moved here, the three of them returned from a very enjoyable night out at the theatre. Mary came up the stairs, there was a scream and she collapsed, dying in Dickens's arms the next day. She was seventeen. The impact on Dickens was enormous. For the first time ever in his professional career as a writer, he failed to meet the printer's deadline for that month's instalments of *Oliver Twist* and *The Pickwick Papers*. He simply couldn't do it.

The impact of Mary's death was longer-lasting than that: the heroines in Dickens's works tend from this point on to be about seventeen years old, with many of them dying. The most immediate was Rose Maylie in *Oliver Twist* who became seriously ill in the episode Dickens was writing shortly after Mary Hogarth died. This was a tragedy that Charles Dickens would carry with him the rest of his life.

The Study in which Dickens finished *The Pickwick Papers* whilst working at the same time on *Oliver Twist*, which demonstrated both his characteristically phenomenal energy as well as his ability to work on several projects simultaneously. He also wrote *Nicholas Nickleby* here, the novel which really propelled him to enormous popularity, as well as starting work on *Barnaby Rudge*. In addition, he also continued unchecked with all his other inexhaustible output as a writer: he contributed articles for *Bentley's Miscellany,* which he also edited; he wrote *Sketches of Young Gentlemen*; as Boz, he edited the *Memoirs of Joseph Grimaldi*, following the death of the most famous clown of the British stage; and he wrote *The Lamplighter*, a comedy for his very dear friend, William Charles Macready, the great actor-manager of Covent Garden Theatre.

He always valued highly his occupation as a journalist as providing one of the most important kinds of writing, since it sharpened his ability to write economically, using the least number of specific words to get a lot said in a very short space. It also gave him a very sensitive ear for names, accents, voices and the accuracy of different kinds of speech which he could store away to be used perhaps years on in the future.

Displays on the walls of the Study are also testimony to the extraordinary reaction to the death of Charles Dickens in all kinds of different art forms. Paintings include 'The Empty Chair' by Sir Luke Fildes, a graphic response following soon after Dickens's death and the elaborate 'Dickens's Dream' by RW Buss, begun after Dickens's death and remaining unfinished when Buss died in 1875, showing the author in his chair, surrounded by images of the characters he created – one of the most popular exhibits at Doughty Street.

*Paul and Florence Dombey.*

*Above: Part of Dickens's dream*

*Opposite page: Other images from Doughty Street*

# Oliver Twist

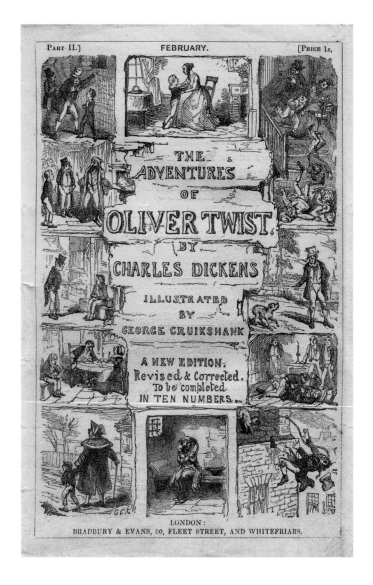

Very near to Clerkenwell Green, in *Oliver Twist*, whilst thoughtfully browsing through a bookshop's stall, Mr. Brownlow is spotted by the Artful Dodger, Charley Bates and Oliver as they *'were just emerging from a narrow court not far from the open square in Clerkinwell, which is yet called, by some strange perversion of terms "The Green"'* and, to Oliver's dismay, they proceeded to pick his pocket.

Later on, Mr Bumble, speaking of an impending legal action, advises Mrs Mann that, *'The Clerkinwell Sessions have brought it upon themselves, Ma'am,' replied Mr Bumble; 'and if the Clerkinwell Sessions find that they come off worse than expected, the Clerkinwell Sessions have only themselves to thank.'*

In Saffron Hill, London EC1 can be found the site of Fagin's Lair in *Oliver Twist*. It was called Field Lane at the time Dickens imagined Fagin's occupancy there. Although much has been rebuilt after being heavily bombed during the war, it nevertheless retains its sinister atmosphere; and it's easy to imagine the Artful Dodger, Charley Bates and the other urchins making their way home after a day's picking of pockets.

The One Tun public house, in Saffron Hill, makes the claim that it was the inspiration for The Three Cripples in *Oliver Twist*. This might be true, but, like so many locations, one can never be entirely certain. Charles Dickens is a great writer not an urban topographer.

*Opposite page top: The Green Clerkenwell, London EC1*
*Bottom left: The Clerkenwell Sessions*
*Bottom right: The One Tun, Saffron Hill, London EC1*

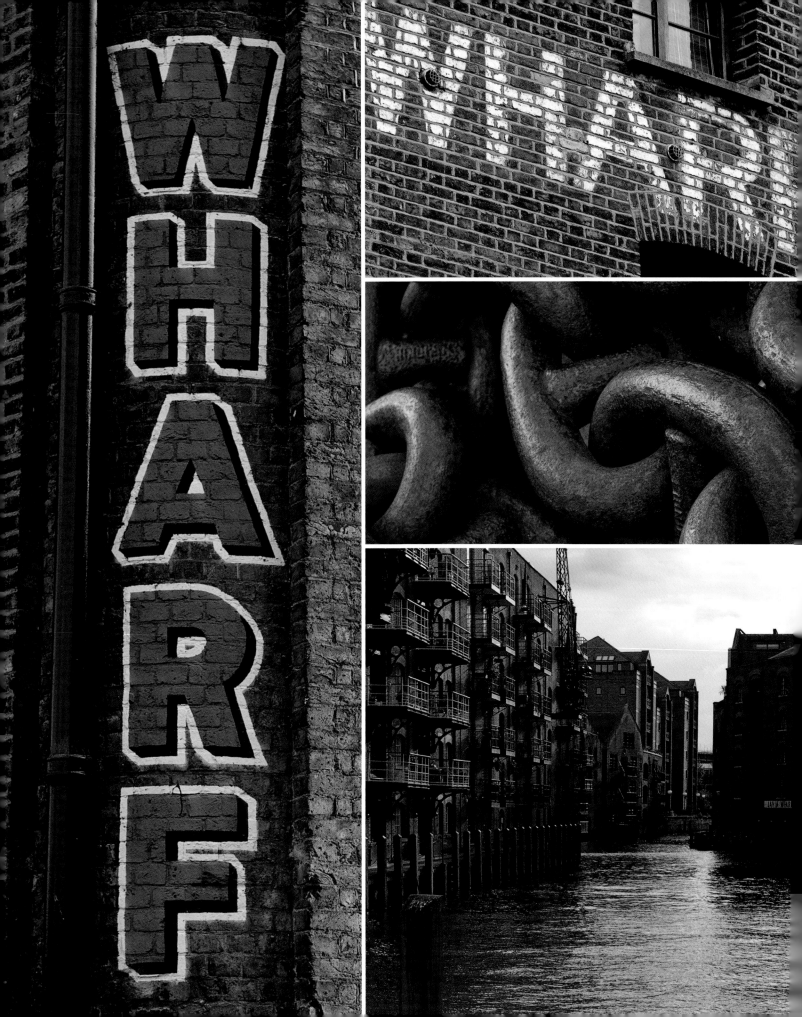

Dickens immortalised Jacob's Island in *Oliver Twist*. It was there that Bill Sikes met his gruesome end in Folly Ditch.

In 1849, *The Morning Chronicle* described Jacob's Island as 'The very capital of cholera' and 'The Venice of drains'. However an ever more brutally penetrating description comes from Dickens himself:

*'Near to that part of the Thames on which the church at Rotherhithe abuts, where the buildings on the banks are dirtiest and the vessels on the river blackest with the dust of colliers and the smoke of close-built low-roofed houses, there exists the filthiest, the strangest, the most extraordinary of the many localities that are hidden in London, wholly unknown, even by name, to the great mass of its inhabitants.*

*Crazy wooden galleries common to the backs of half a dozen houses, with holes from which to look upon the slime beneath; windows, broken and patched, with poles thrust out, on which to dry the linen that is never there; rooms so small, so filthy, so confined, that the air would seem too tainted even for the dirt and squalor which they shelter; wooden chambers thrusting themselves out above the mud, and threatening to fall into it, as some have done; dirt-besmeared walls and decaying foundations; every repulsive lineament of poverty, every loathsome indication of filth, rot, and garbage; all these ornament the banks of Folly Ditch.*

*In Jacob's Island, the warehouses are roofless and empty; the walls are crumbling down; the windows are windows no more; the doors are falling into the streets, the chimneys are blackened, but they yield no smoke. Thirty or forty years ago, before losses and chancery suits came upon it, it was a thriving place; but now it is a desolate island indeed. The houses have no owners; they are broken open, and entered upon by those who have the courage; and there they live, and there they die. They must have powerful motives for a secret residence, or be reduced to a destitute condition indeed, who seek a refuge in Jacob's Island.'*

*Above and opposite page: The site of Jacob's Island, London SE1*

*Opposite page: Holborn Viaduct today, London EC1*
*Oliver Twist trudged along behind Bill Sikes at Holborn Viaduct, on their way to the crib at Chertsey. 'Crib' was then thieves' slang for a house*

At the clock of St. Andrew's Church, Oliver was told *'now young un! hard upon seven! you must step out. Come, don't lag behind already, Lazylegs!'*

This began a journey of well over 20 miles. At Hyde Park Corner, Oliver and Bill Sikes were able to hitch a lift as far as Isleworth on a cart bound for Hounslow.

*'As they passed the different mile-stones, Oliver wondered, more and more, where his companion meant to take him. Kensington, Hammersmith, Chiswick, Kew Bridge, Brentford, were all passed; and yet they went on as steadily as if they had only just begun their journey. At length they came to a public house called The Coach and Horse…'*

The Coach and Horses, Isleworth, Middlesex, is still there today, on the outer edge of Syon Park. Syon House, reputedly the second largest house in greater London after Buckingham Palace, is adorned with the Lion taken from Northumberland House at Charing Cross after its demolition. This lion was very well known to Dickens as a boy, and he mentioned it in *Gone Astray*.

Even with the lift of a cart ride, the walk for all of them would still have been considerable, and especially difficult for the little legs of a child. They carried on through Isleworth to Twickenham and then on to Hampton. Twickenham was omitted from the very first edition of *Oliver Twist* in volume form. It appeared in *Bentley's Miscellany* in serial form. They carried on to Shepperton via Sunbury eventually arriving at Chertsey.

This journey is so meticulously detailed in *Oliver Twist*, almost to guide book standard, it leads one to suppose that Dickens actually walked the route, noting its details as he went.

After everything went wrong during the bungled robbery, the wounded Oliver attempted to retrace their steps for the return journey, an enormous distance for a fit and healthy young boy, let alone an injured one.

Nancy was unfortunate enough to be overheard by Noah Claypole making her disclosures to Mr Brownlow at the bottom of the original London Bridge. This would lead to her violent murder.

The London Bridge used by Dickens in the novel is the Rennie Bridge which opened in 1831 and was built 1824-1831, replacing the older bridge which dated from 13th century. Dickens used this as a venue for many of his characters: Riah in *Our Mutual Friend*, Mr. Haredale in *Barnaby Rudge*, Nadget in *Martin Chuzzlewit*, as well as David Copperfield making his first acquaintance with London.

The present bridge was built 1967-72, replacing the Rennie Bridge which was sold to the American entrepreneur Robert P. McCulloch in 1968 who mistakenly thought he was buying the far more magnificent Tower Bridge instead for the then huge sum of $2 million. The bridge was dismantled stone by stone and reassembled at Lake Havasu City, Arizona. Nonetheless, today it is the state's second most popular tourist attraction after the Grand Canyon.

LONDON
BRIDGE

# Nicholas Nickleby

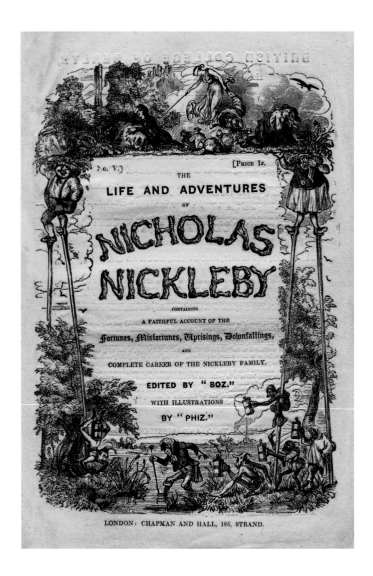

Encouraged by the success of his exposition of the injustices of the workhouse in *Oliver Twist*, with the vitality that was to become his trademark, Dickens turned his attentions to the abuse of the young in school, as his next creation, *Nicholas Nickleby*, began to take shape.

Dickens was always capable of great outrage and anger at social abuses and inequalities, and a particular national scandal in the early nineteenth century was to strike a special note for him concerning the ill-treatment of children. There was much in the air of the late 1830s about the Yorkshire Schools, which were responsible for a particular kind of abuse and, as such, were untypical of the whole education 'system' such as it was before 1870.

There is no doubt that some of the schools were good, honest establishments. Equally there were others that were run by rogues and charlatans for profit, and subjected the pupils to regimes of brutality and horror, resulting in disease, blindness and even death.

*At the time Dickens visited this area, it was in Yorkshire;*
*but as a result of subsequent boundary changes, it is now*
*in County Durham*

Having learned of appalling instances of ill-treatment, he travelled incognito to Bowes with his illustrator, Hablôt Knight Browne (Phiz), to research the subject.

Dickens was helped in this endeavour by Charles Smithson of Smithson and Dunn, a friend from London, who had later moved back to Malton, Yorkshire, after his father died. He provided letters of introduction to a lawyer in Barnard Castle, Richard Barnes, whom Dickens would mention in his preface to *Nicholas Nickleby* and upon whom he drew for the character of John Browdie in the novel. Barnes, in turn, gave him details of a number of schools in the area.

Smithson lived at Easthorpe Hall in Malton, where Dickens would stay whilst writing *Martin Chuzzlewit*. His office in Chancery Lane in Malton is thought to have been used by Dickens as the model for Ebenezer Scrooge's counting house. Smithson is also mentioned in the preface to *Barnaby Rudge* as the Yorkshire friend *'who discovered an older and more gifted raven at a village public-house, which he prevailed upon the landlord to part with for a consideration, and sent to me.'* The raven became the inspiration for Grip.

With such connections, Malton now has its own Charles Dickens Society as well as a Dickens Festival.

*Opposite page: The three*
*coaching inns at Greta Bridge*
*Top: This is the George and New*
*Inn where Dickens stayed. Part*
*of the building was destroyed in*
*a fire*
*Bottom right: The Morritt Arms*

*Above: The Greta Bridge*

Dickens and Phiz travelled for two days by stagecoach from London, through a bleak midwinter landscape, stopping at Grantham for the first night. They alighted on the second day in Greta Bridge shortly before midnight. As in Dickens's day, it remains a small village today. It was, nevertheless, then a major hub for stagecoaches, travelling both north and south. At the time of Dickens's visit, there were three coaching inns. Only one, The Morritt Arms, still retains its original function, providing rest and sustenance for the weary traveller. In its bar, they continue to honour Dickens and his works to this day.

From the George and New Inn, Greta Bridge, where Dickens stayed, he wrote to Catherine, *'We have had for breakfast toasts, cakes, a Yorkshire pie, a piece of beef about the size and much the shape of my portmanteau, tea, coffee, ham and eggs - and are now going to look about us.'*

*Above: The mural of Dickens characters was painted by John Gillroy in 1946.*
*He had been commissioned to paint a portrait of the Morritt's owner and on*
*discovering the Dickens connection he painted this in his own time.*
*Gillroy is best known for his iconic posters for Guinness, the Irish stout*

*Opposite page:*
*Top left: The site of the King's Head,*
*Barnard Castle, County Durham*
*Bottom left: Master Humpherys clock shop*
*Right: The site where the shop relocated*

Following their breakfast, Dickens and Phiz made their way the short distance to Barnard Castle. There, they stayed at the King's Head Hotel, now a residential care home. Just across the road was 9-13 Market Place, the premises of the town's clock maker, Thomas Humphrey - a name and trade which Dickens would use for another story, *Master Humphrey's Clock*. The shop later moved just down the road.

In *Nicholas Nickleby*, Newman Noggs says, in a letter to Nicholas, *'if you should go near Barnard Castle, there is good ale at the King's Head. Say you know me and I am sure they will not charge you for it.'*

Posing as the friend of a widowed mother who wanted to place her child in such an institution, with introduction letters provided by Smithson, Dickens arranged to visit the Bowes Academy School for Gentlemen – headmaster, William Shaw, the template for the character of Mr Squeers in *Nicholas Nickleby*.

As well as providing utterly squalid living conditions and very little education, several of Shaw's pupils had actually gone blind due to '*gross neglect*'. It is difficult to imagine these attractive homes were once the blueprint for that infamous establishment known as 'Dotheboys Hall'.

Dickens had read of two cases in the courts, from October 1823 (Ockerby v Shaw and Jones v Shaw), where William Shaw had been found responsible for boys going blind from neglect. William Jones, aged eleven, recalled during the case against Shaw, how the pupils washed in a horse trough, shared two filthy towels, ate small rations and slept five to a bed in a thirty-bed dormitory. The boys' first job every morning was to de-flea their beds with quills. '*If they did not catch all the fleas, they were beaten,*' the court report stated. Nine months after Jones had been at the school, his

sight became so poor that he could not see to write. Because of this, as punishment, the boy was sent to the wash-house where he remained for a month, by which time he was completely blind, as were nine other boys who shared the wash-house with him.

William Shaw was found guilty of gross neglect and was forced to pay £300 damages to the parents of the boys. On the following day another action against Shaw was withdrawn after the very first witness and Shaw agreed to pay another £300 – in total around £25,000 in today's money. The judge also said, however, that he found nothing to impeach the general conduct of Mr Shaw in the management of the school, thereby allowing him to continue '*educating*' boys.

*Above: Dotheboys Hall, Bowes, County Durham*

*Opposite page: The doorway that hundreds of wretched boys would pass through to be taught by William Shaw. Some would never walk back through*

*William Shaw's professional card read –*

At Bowes Academy near Greta Bridge, Yorkshire; youth are carefully instructed in the English, Latin and Greek languages, Writing, Common and Decimal Arithmetic, Book-Keeping, Mensuration, Surveying, Geometry, Geography, and Navigation, with the most useful branches of mathematics, and are provided with Board, Clothes, and every necessary at twenty Guineas per annum each. No vacations except by Parent's desire.

N.B. The French language Two Guineas per annum extra.

Mr Shaw attends at the George and Blue Boar, High Holborn, the three first weeks in the months of January and July.

'Past seven, Nickleby,' said Mr Squeers.

'Has morning come already?' asked Nicholas, sitting up in bed.

'Ah! that has it,' replied Squeers, 'and ready iced too. Now, Nickleby, come; tumble up, will you?'

Nicholas needed no further admonition, but 'tumbled up' at once, and proceeded to dress himself by the light of the taper, which Mr Squeers carried in his hand.

'Here's a pretty go,' said that gentleman; 'the pump's froze.'

'Indeed!' said Nicholas, not much interested in the intelligence.

'Yes,' replied Squeers. 'You can't wash yourself this morning.'

'Not wash myself!' exclaimed Nicholas.

'No, not a bit of it,' rejoined Squeers tartly. 'So you must be content with giving yourself a dry polish till we break the ice in the well, and can get a bucketful out for the boys. Don't stand staring at me, but do look sharp, will you?'

*Left: William Shaw's original pump*
*Opposite page: Most of the area of the school classroom was knocked down.*
*Only this section remains*

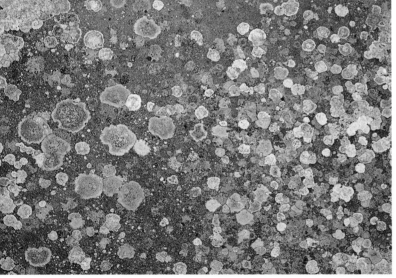

Hidden under a tree, there is a grave - that of George Ashton Taylor who died whilst a pupil at the Academy. When Dickens saw this, he wrote:

*'The country for miles around was covered, when I was there, with deep snow. There is an old Church near the school, and the first grave-stone I stumbled on that dreary winter afternoon was placed above the grave of a boy, eighteen long years old, who had died -- suddenly, the inscription said; I suppose his heart broke -- the Camel falls down "suddenly" when they heap the last load upon his back -- died at that wretched place. I think his ghost put Smike into my head, upon the spot.'*

Smike was the wretched boy whom Nicholas Nickleby had befriended.

Shaw had been warned by colleagues from other schools that a young writer from London was trying to find out more about the Yorkshire schools for a book he was writing. Shaw, suspecting Dickens was the writer, refused to allow him inside, but not before Dickens had noted that Shaw had *'a slight scale covering the pupil of one of his eyes'* which gave him a vivid detail to work up into the character of Squeers who *'had but one eye, while the popular prejudice runs in favour of two.'*

Dickens also saw the exterior of the school building, which, in the novel, became *'a long cold-looking house, one story high, with a few straggling outbuildings behind, and a barn and stables adjoining.'*

The visit was sufficient to help Dickens create a work of genius that had a far reaching impact, both for his own career and to help right a great wrong.

*Opposite page, top left: As grasping even in death as he was in life, William Shaw's head stone is unsurprisingly larger than that of anyone else in St Gile's Churchyard in Bowes*
*Bottom left: The gravestone states that George Ashton Taylor was actually nineteen, not eighteen. A rare inaccuracy by Dickens*

Ralph Nickleby, who was responsible for sending his nephew to Dotheboys Hall, lived in a spacious house in Golden Square. Newman Noggs, Ralph's clerk and Nicholas's confidant, lodged nearby.

Dickens used this setting again in *David Copperfield* when David and Martha Endell discover Little Em'ly, a niece of Mr Peggotty, near Golden Square.

In the summer of 1838, Dickens stayed at Ailsa Park Villas in Twickenham, during the writing of *Nicholas Nickleby*. At that time, this was very much a countryside retreat; today, it's simply an extension of London.

In the same novel, there is a duel between Sir Mulberry Hawk and Lord Verisopht which takes place in *'one of the meadows opposite Twickenham by the riverside'*, leading to the death of the young lord. This was very probably at the bottom of Richmond Hill.

Dickens visited the Star and Garter Hotel at the top of Richmond Hill many times, not only for family outings and birthdays but also for the celebration of the launch of a number of his novels, including *David Copperfield*, which was a colossal triumph. The Star and Garter Hotel was replaced by the current building.

*Left: Possibly the inspiration for Ralph Nickleby's house, Golden Square, London W1*

*Opposite page, top left: Ailsa Park Villas, Twickenham, Middlesex*
*Middle right: The Star and Garter, Richmond, Surrey*
*Bottom: Meadow opposite Twickenham, in Richmond*

Eel Pie Island, located in the middle of the river Thames at Twickenham, Middlesex, even now evokes an atmosphere that Dickens would have recognised.

In *Nicholas Nickleby* –

*'It had come to pass, that afternoon, that Miss Morleena Kenwigs had received an invitation to repair next day, per steamer from Westminster Bridge, unto the Eel Pie Island at Twickenham: there to make merry upon a cold collation, bottled beer, shrub, and shrimps, and to dance in the open air to the music of a locomotive band.'*

*Above right: The land-based boat, now used by an artist, is a very modern echo to the home Dickens imagined for Mr. Peggotty in David Copperfield*
*Following spread: Eel Pie Island, Twickenham, Middlesex, today*

113

# Devonshire Terrace

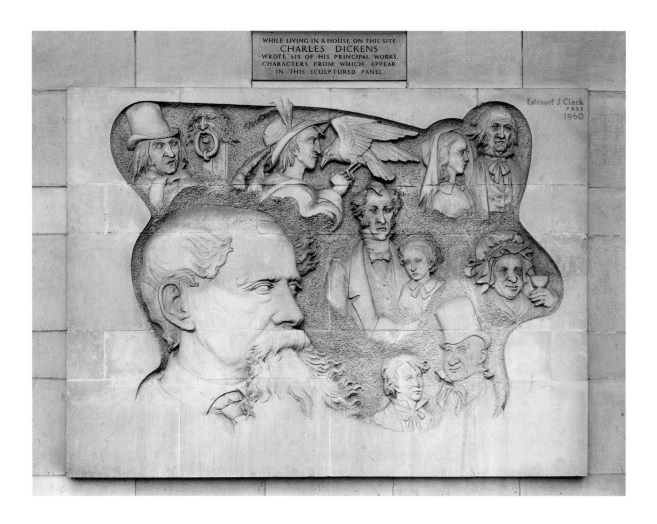

WHILE LIVING IN A HOUSE ON THIS SITE
**CHARLES DICKENS**
WROTE SIX OF HIS PRINCIPAL WORKS,
CHARACTERS FROM WHICH APPEAR
IN THIS SCULPTURED PANEL

Estcourt J Clack
FRBS
1960

*Dickens's Characters Top left:
A Christmas Carol, Barnaby
Rudge, The Old Curiosity Shop
Middle: Dombey and Son;
Martin Chuzzlewit
Bottom: David Copperfield*

*The mural is on Marylebone
High Street, London NW1*

In December 1839, Charles and his growing family moved to 1 Devonshire Terrace, Regents Park. This magnificent home propelled him into residing in the smartest area of his life so far, reflecting his new-found wealth and popularity.

Here, between 1839 and 1851, he worked tirelessly, producing *The Old Curiosity Shop, Barnaby Rudge, Martin Chuzzlewit, A Christmas Carol, Dombey and Son* and *David Copperfield*. These novels alone would incontestably establish Dickens as one of the world's foremost novelists. He described the house as a *'frightful first class family mansion involving awful responsibilities.'* Nevertheless, it provided an ambience he loved and it became his most favourite home.

The gardens of 1 Devonshire Terrace when Dickens was there were between the house and the Marylebone Road, offering some screening from what was already a busy road. The entrance to the house was in what is now Marylebone High Street and is marked now by a large plaque and quotation. There is also a small quantity of low wall which is original and survived the demolition in 1958-9.

# The Old Curiosity Shop

THE OLD
CURIOSITY SHOP

BY
CHARLES DICKENS

ILLUSTRATED BY
PHIZ

LONDON:
HAZELL, WATSON & VINEY, LTD.

The term, 'old curiosity shop', was in general use in Dickens's time and would not simply have been the title of one specific establishment. As Dickens says, such a shop was *'one of those receptacles for old and curious things'* and describes some of the objects as looking as if they were *'designed in dreams.'*

At the end of *The Old Curiosity Shop*, Dickens himself writes, *'The old house had been long ago pulled down, and a fine broad road was in its place.'* Nevertheless, it has exercised many people over many years to try to locate it. This misses the point as Dickens is less interested in locating the place than in using it as a kind of representational image for London.

Although several locations in various towns and cities in England have lain claim to being home to his original inspiration, such as that illustrated here, this is decidedly not the original model. Nevertheless, it most definitely is a curiosity and an increasingly rare example of a shop dating from 1567 and gives a sense of what this area would have been like before Kingsway was constructed between 1900 and 1905. It is also one with which Dickens would have been decidedly familiar.

*Right and over: The Old Curiosity Shop Portsmouth Street, London WC2*

# Barnaby Rudge

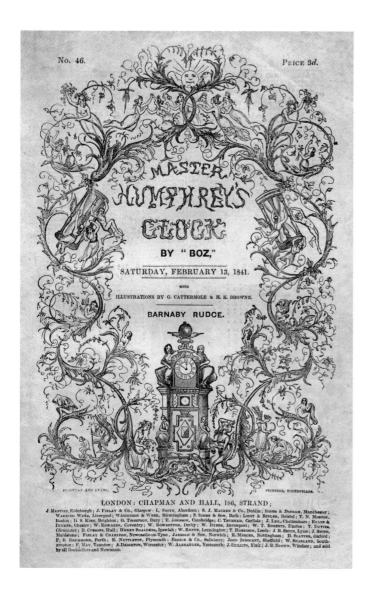

The heart of the story in *Barnaby Rudge* begins and ends with one building, The Maypole Inn, the inspiration for which is the still fully-functioning Kings Head Public House in Chigwell, Essex. '*Chigwell, my dear fellow, is the greatest place on earth. Name your day for going*', Dickens wrote to his great friend, John Forster. '*Such a delicious old inn opposite the churchyard - such a lovely ride - such beautiful forest scenery - such an out of the way, rural place – such a sexton! I say again, name your day.*' Having taken up such a persuasive offer, Forster subsequently noted that Dickens's '*promise was exceeded by our enjoyment; and his delight in the double recognition, of himself and of Barnaby, by the landlord of the nice old inn, far exceeding any pride he would have taken in what the world thinks the sort of honour.*'

*Left:* Barnaby Rudge *was originally published in the 'Master Humphrey's Clock' periodical*

*Opposite page: Ye Olde Kings Head, Chigwell, Essex, formally The Maypole Inn*

# John Forster's House

A short walk up the road from 'The Old Curiosity Shop' in Portsmouth Street is 58 Lincoln's Inn Fields. This was once the home of John Forster, a man Dickens had met on Christmas Day 1836, who had become his closest friend and who, one day, would become his official biographer.

On the 3rd December 1844, Dickens gave a reading for a few friends of one of a series of Christmas Books called *The Chimes* which he had written whilst staying in Genoa in Italy. This was the first time he had ever read his work to an audience other than his family.

The previous year, he had written perhaps his most popular Christmas story of all, *A Christmas Carol*.

John Forster's home also became the fictional home of the sinister lawyer, Mr. Tulkinghorn in *Bleak House*.

*'Here in a large house, formerly a house of state, lives Mr. Tulkinghorn. It is let off in sets of chambers now; and in those shrunken fragments of its greatness, lawyers lie like maggots in nuts.'*

It was in here that Mr. Tulkinghorn was murdered.

*Above: John Forster's House, Lincoln's Inn Field, London WC2*
*Opposite page, bottom left: The room where Dickens first read to an audience*

# A Christmas Carol

*Scrooge's third Visitor*

Dickens is often described as the man who invented our modern Christmas through his stories, re-discovering old English customs that may well otherwise have died out. In *A Christmas Carol*, it was at the Royal Exchange in London that Scrooge was to be found daily amongst other men of business.

*'Business!' cried the Ghost, wringing its hands again. 'Mankind was my business. The common welfare was my business; charity, mercy, forbearance, and benevolence, were, all, my business. The dealings of my trade were but a drop of water in the comprehensive ocean of my business!'*

The Royal Exchange also saw service as a venue for Pip and Herbert Pocket in *Great Expectations*, Quilp in *The Old Curiosity Shop* and Flintwich in *Little Dorrit*.

*Opposite page: The Royal Exchange, Bank, London EC3*

THE EARTH IS
THE LORD'S
AND THE FULNESS
THEREOF

R · XIII · CONDITVM · ANNO · VICTORIAE

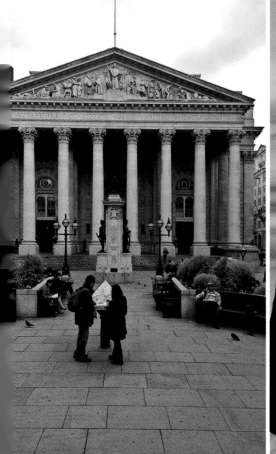

# SIGHTSEEING

Once Scrooge had survived his extraordinary night with the three Christmas spirits, the chimes from the clock of St. Dunstan-in-the-West Church in Fleet Street would have been amongst those that awoke him to his new life. Although Dickens doesn't locate it and describes *'the churches ringing out the lustiest peals he had ever heard'*, it is really an amalgam of London church bells on Christmas morning and hard to differentiate one from another, there being several churches around the Cornhill area.

Of all the public readings Dickens would come to adapt, *A Christmas Carol* was by far the most popular of all with audiences.

St. Dunstan's also provided the same clock that David Copperfield and his aunt stopped by in order to watch the 'giants' strike the bells at noon.

During the writing of *A Christmas Carol*, Dickens would walk through the streets of London for many miles, working out the story in his mind. Dickens was a prolific walker. In his early life, it was out of necessity; but later on, when he could afford less arduous means of transport, he still strode huge distances - Durham to Sunderland, Yarmouth to Lowestoft and London to Rochester.

*Opposite page and above: St. Dunstan-in-the-West Church, Fleet Street, London WC2*

# London Observations

Dickens was captivated by the area known as Seven Dials, a vicinity he would often explore, but with great apprehension. Today, it boasts expensive clothes shops, five star hotels and coffee bars; but in his day, it was a dangerous locality with a hotchpotch of alleyways, all meeting at this point, and all housing pawnbrokers, gin palaces and the like, and populated by a truly gruesome assortment of rogues and scoundrels.

Dickens was both appalled and fascinated by this area. He wrote of its *'dirty men and filthy women, squalid children, fluttering shuttlecocks, noisy battledores, recking pipes, bad fruit, more than doubtful oysters, attenuated cats, depressed dogs.'*

London is renowned the world over for its public houses or pubs, serving beer and all manner of alcoholic drinks. But in Dickens's day, gin was very much the order of the day, and Seven Dials was full of gin palaces. Each would house vast barrels, with names on their labels such as *The Cream of The Valley, The No Mistake, The Real Knock Me Down, The Regular Flare Up, Old Tom, Young Tom*. And the winning advertising slogan of the day was *'Drunk for a penny, Dead Drunk for twopence.'*

*Above: George Cruickshank's observation of a Gin Palace*

*Opposite page: Seven Dials, London WC2*
*Following spread: The alleyways of London*

# Martin Chuzzlewit

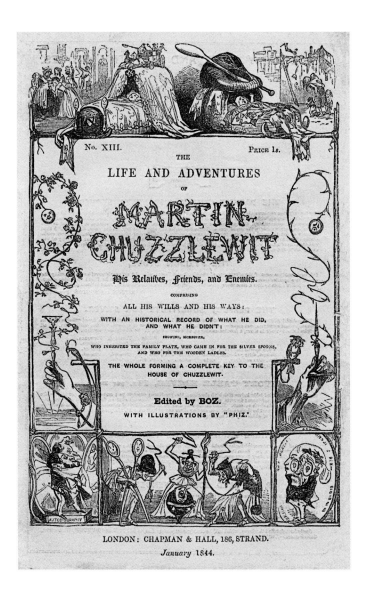

No. XIII.                              PRICE 1s.

THE

## LIFE AND ADVENTURES

OF

## MARTIN CHUZZLEWIT

His Relatives, Friends, and Enemies.

COMPRISING

ALL HIS WILLS AND HIS WAYS:

WITH AN HISTORICAL RECORD OF WHAT HE DID,
AND WHAT HE DIDN'T:

SHOWING, MOREOVER,

WHO INHERITED THE FAMILY PLATE, WHO CAME IN FOR THE SILVER SPOONS,
AND WHO FOR THE WOODEN LADLES.

THE WHOLE FORMING A COMPLETE KEY TO THE
HOUSE OF CHUZZLEWIT.

Edited by BOZ.

WITH ILLUSTRATIONS BY "PHIZ."

LONDON: CHAPMAN & HALL, 186, STRAND.
*January* 1844.

Guided by his recurrent restlessness to benefit from new surroundings, Dickens lodged at Cobley's Farm in Finchley whilst writing part of *Martin Chuzzlewit* which appeared in weekly instalments between 1843-44. Now part of Greater London, in Dickens's time, like Ailsa Park Villas, this was out in the country. Today, a plaque on the current site commemorates this stay.

Also in *Martin Chuzzlewit,* it was observed of Tom Pinch, *'in his guileless distrust of London'* that *'The Man in the Monument was quite as mysterious a being to Tom as the Man in the Moon.'*

M Todgers's Boarding House, proprietor Mrs Todgers, where Pecksniff and his daughters stay when visiting London, is situated in the vicinity of The Monument. *'Surely there never was, in any other borough, city or hamlet in the world, such a singular sort of place as Todgers's.'* However, *'Nobody ever found Todgers's on a verbal direction, though given within a few minutes' walk of it.'*

*Opposite page, top left: Cobley's Farm, Finchley, in Dickens's day and below how it looks today*
*Bottom left: Fountain Court in Temple is where the romance between John Westlock and Ruth Pinch commences*
*Right: The Monument, London EC3*

ON THIS SPOT WAS
SITUATED COBLEY'S FARM,
WHERE
CHARLES DICKENS
LIVED IN 1843 WHILE
WRITING MARTIN CHUZZLEWIT.
IT IS RECORDED THAT
DURING HIS WALKS WITH
FORSTER AND MACLISE
AND HARD BY THE HOUSE

# Dombey and Son

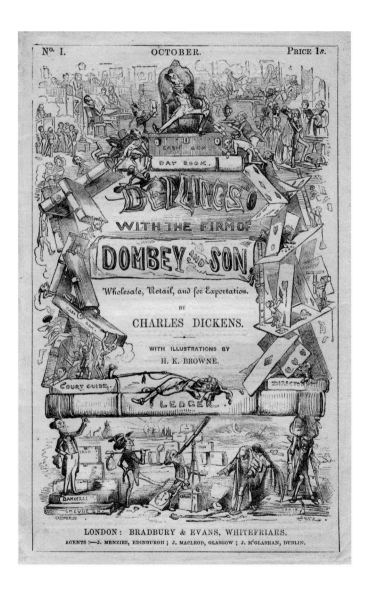

Dickens left England in 1844-5 to spend time in Italy and Switzerland. There, the formulation for a new novel was taking shape, *Dombey and Son*, which he wrote outside Lausanne, on the shores of Lake Geneva in Switzerland. However, whilst away, he did comment that he had plucked himself out of his proper soil by leaving London and would not be able to write anything until he walked again through his beloved streets, which he referred to as *'that magic lantern.'*

Located close to his house in Devonshire Terrace stands St. Marylebone Parish Church which Dickens put to great use in *Dombey and Son*. He used it for little Paul Dombey's christening, Mr. Dombey's doomed marriage to Edith Granger and, following young Paul's death, the child was buried in the churchyard there.

*Opposite page: St Marylebone Parish Church, London NW1*

After Switzerland and a further three months exploring Paris, the family returned to London when Charley had gone down with scarlet fever. They were unable to occupy 1 Devonshire Terrace because it was still leased out whilst they were travelling in Europe; so they found accommodation at 1 Chester Place, Regents Park, the address which appears on Dickens's correspondence written between 8th March 1847 and 24th June 1847 (See Pilgrim *Letters* volume 5).

He then stayed for a few days at the Athenaeum before going down to Broadstairs for the summer.

On 23rd August, he wrote to Forster on returning to Devonshire Terrace. *'Here we are in the noble old premises'* prior to going back to Broadstairs until the end of September.

Between 1846-8, *Dombey and Son* appeared in monthly parts.

*Opposite page and right:*
*Chester Place, Regents Park*

# The Railways

Dickens was always possessed with a recurrent restlessness to move on to new surroundings, whether that involved writing or simply living. On his own admission, idleness unsettled him. Even when he was on holiday, he continued to store up observations as raw-material for future works.

Later on in life, his reading engagements offered him a much welcomed opportunity to travel throughout the British Isles and beyond. At such a time of transition, from stagecoach to rail, he absolutely loved it. Indeed, so enthusiastic was his use of this new mode of transport that, on 12<sup>th</sup> September 1858, he wrote to his sister-in-law, Georgina Hogarth, following a journey from Harrogate to Scarborough, *'I seem to have been doing nothing all my life, but riding in railway carriages and reading.'*

*Opposite and following spread: Bluebell Railway, Sheffield Park, Sussex*

# Highgate Cemetery

On 2<sup>nd</sup> September 1848, after a lengthy decline in her health, Charles's sister, Fanny, died. She had been diagnosed with tuberculosis after collapsing at a party in Manchester, and Charles had found lodgings for her and her husband in the village of Hornsey, where he visited her almost daily. At her funeral, in Highgate Cemetery, it was said, *'Mr. Dickens appeared to feel it very deeply.'*

Perhaps it was Fanny's death and thoughts of his own mortality that prompted the idea for his next and most semi-autobiographical novel, *David Copperfield*.

*Top right: The Dickens family grave*
*Opposite and following spread:*
*Highgate Cemetery, London N6*

# David Copperfield

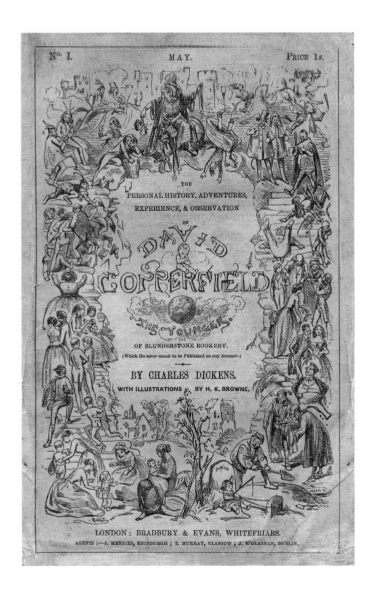

Dickens had visited Broadstairs on holiday in August 1837. It was a place to which he was to return many times in subsequent years. In September 1839, Charles and Catherine, later joined by their children, stayed at 40 Albion Street, now part of the Albion Hotel. He used this visit to complete writing *Nicholas Nickleby,* which he finished on 20th September 1839.

However, for many people the novel most associated with the town is *David Copperfield.*

Dickens occupied several properties on his visits to Broadstairs, including 12 High Street - now number 31, from which he wrote to John Forster, *'I have seen ladies and gentlemen walking upon the earth in slippers of buff, and pickling themselves in the sea in complete suits of the same.'* So enamoured was he with Broadstairs that, over the following fifteen years, he spent all but two summers there. Dickens affectionately referred to it as *'our English watering place.'*

What is now the Dickens House Museum was formerly the home of Mary Pearson Strong, a woman who was in her late sixties when the young, handsome Dickens, aged twenty-seven, first met her. Visiting with her regularly on his subsequent trips to Broadstairs, he obviously admired this rather elderly, stiff-in-the-back lady with a kind heart, and they developed a friendship, often taking tea together in her parlour.

This friendship lead to both Mary and the home in which she lived becoming his inspiration for Betsey Trotwood in *David Copperfield*. Her parlour and the outside of the house would one day appear in Chapter 13 of *David Copperfield,* with Betsey meeting David, her exhausted nephew, on her garden path and bringing him into her parlour to tend to his health.

Whilst taking tea, Dickens became used to Mary Pearson Strong's incensed cry, *'Donkeys!'*, a watchword which Betsey Trotwood would also take up in his story. Mary took great offence at the donkey boys going across what she considered to be her property. It was not so much the donkeys she objected to, but rather, the boys themselves, who could be any age, shape, size or temperament.

*Top: Staff at Dickens House Museum*
*Broadstairs, Kent*
*Bottom: Objects in the museum*

The beautiful bay at Broadstairs, known in Dickens's time as Main Bay. One can imagine Dickens watching the people on the beach below running about in 'suits of buff', as he described it. This was during the very early Victorian period; and the bathing suit really didn't come into its own until the beginning of the 1850s, so it would have been very natural for people to bath in that manner.

Bleak House – originally called Fort House, was built in 1801 as a residence for the Fort captain during the Napoleonic Wars, though not initially built with its castellated appearance. Thomas Barry, the owner in the early 20th century, 'added a wing to the building, and made the exterior of a uniform Tudor style.' Although Dickens stayed and wrote there many times, he wouldn't know it as it stands today since it wasn't actually restored as it is now until 32 years after he died.

It's now called 'Bleak House' after the book. Although Dickens wrote part of David Copperfield there, not a word of Bleak House was written in or about Broadstairs.

The Royal Albion Hotel was then called Ballards Hotel where Dickens stayed on many occasions, looking out over the sea for inspiration for his writing. We know he approved of the view by writing his letters from 'Hotel Ballard, Broadstairs sur Mer.'

He used to invite people to come to Broadstairs for 'the sun, the sea and the air'; and he talked about the sun sparkling on the water. He was a regular visitor, over a period of fifteen years, from 1837 when he first came, to a flying visit in 1859.

Dickens never stayed in any one place to write a complete novel, often working on the move.

Dickens talked of Broadstairs as being a rather 'nobby place' - with dukes and duchesses riding in their carriages and elderly gentlemen and ancient ladies sitting on the benches - as opposed to Margate and Ramsgate, which were considered vastly inferior – they were the commoner places.

LEE AULT

**Curator, Dickens House Museum Broadstairs and Joint Honorary Secretary, International Dickens Fellowship**

CHARLES DICKENS

*Dickens wrote some of his favourite novel, David Copperfield, which appeared in monthly instalments between 1849-50, at Ballard's Hotel, Broadstairs – now the Royal Albion Hotel*

As well as its splendidly evocative parlour, Dickens House Museum also contains numerous original treasures associated with Dickens: such as Dickens's sumptuous writing box, a present from John Forster; Dickens's letters written from or about Broadstairs; prints by 'Phiz'; furniture; costumes; photographs and prints of the author and important events in his life; personal writing materials; as well as the delightful ambience of the house itself. Dickens House Museum is *definitely* an essential visit.

Like any writer, in order to concentrate on assembling the right elements for his characters and stories, Dickens needed quiet. Sometimes however the intruding noises from the holiday atmosphere outside drove Dickens to distraction. On one such occasion, he found that he had a violinist on his doorstep early one morning, obviously screeching away. And there were also German 'Oompah' bands which were becoming quite fashionable.

He wrote to John Forster:

*'Vagrant music is getting to that height here, and is so impossible to be escaped from, that I feel Broadstairs and I must part company in time to come. Unless it pours of rain, I cannot write half-an-hour without the most excruciating organs, fiddles, bells or glee-singers. There is a violin of the most torturing kind under the window now (time, ten in the morning) and an Italian box of music on the steps – both in full blast.'*

Unfortunately he stopped visiting on a regular basis in 1851 because it became too noisy

Throughout his life, Dickens was much attracted to water which figures greatly in his personal life as well as his novels. His life was infused by *'the splash and plop of the tide'* which always ran through his imagination.

*Above: General views of Broadstairs, Kent*

153

Whilst working on *David Copperfield*, in June 1849, Dickens leased a house called 'Winterbourne', now an hotel, at Bonchurch, on the Isle of Wight. It's interesting to note that, in both of the houses in which he worked whilst writing *David Copperfield*, in Broadstairs and on the Isle of Wight, he sat at desks overlooking the sea - the sea, which features so greatly in the novel.

A by-product of his love of all things to do with water was that Dickens became an early exponent of the concept of personal hygiene, bucking the Victorian trend towards filth as a protection, staving off ills. He and his family would frequently bathe in the waterfall showerbath.

Shanklin, Isle of Wight
Monday night sixteenth June 1849

My Dear Kate,
I have not a moment just got back, and the post going out. I have taken a most delightful and beautiful house belonging to White, at Bonchurch; cool, airy, private bathing, everything delicious. I think it's the prettiest place I ever saw in my life, at home or abroad. Anne may begin to dismantle Devonshire Terrace. I have arranged for carriages, luggage, and everything. We shall be home, most probably tomorrow night. If I don't get back before John goes to bed, tell him to leave the iron gate open, that I may be able to ring him up. If anything should occur to detain us until Wednesday, you will not be alarmed.
Best loves to Georgy and the children.
The man with the postbag is swearing in the passage.

 Ever affectionately,

CD

A waterfall on the grounds, which I have arranged with a carpenter to convert into a perpetual shower bath.

Top right and opposite page: Sadly this is the waterfall today, concreted over and hidden by a garage - more of a car wash than a showerbath

156

But this was only a natural progression for Dickens. In London, as a young boy, he often visited this Roman Bath, as did his character, David Copperfield. *'There was an old Roman bath in those days at the bottom of one of the streets out of the Strand - it may still be there - in which I have had many a cold plunge.'*

The Sun Inn, in Sun Street, Canterbury, where Micawber stays in *David Copperfield,* is just one of that novel's many locations associated with the city; and nearly the only one based on an actual building that is still standing. As well as his fictional characters, Dickens himself also often stayed at the Sun Inn.

As for Dickens's standing as a writer amongst his peers, the storm at sea in chapter 55 of *David Copperfield,* which culminates in the drowning of both Ham Peggotty and Steerforth, was Tolstoy's favourite chapter in the whole of fiction.

*Opposite page: The almost forgotten, and hard to locate, Roman Baths, London WC2*
*Right: The Sun Hotel, Canterbury, Kent*

# Tavistock House, Bloomsbury

In 1851, now at the peak of his career and with an ever growing family, the desire for more room prompted Dickens to pay £1,450 (£64,000 today) for the 45 year lease of Tavistock House in Bloomsbury, now the offices of the British Medical Association.

His energies unabated, he also took on the editorship of a new journal called *Household Words* from 1850-59.

Rules Restaurant near Covent Garden was one of the much-loved social venues favoured by Dickens and one popular with most of the leading writers of the day.

Another favourite haunt was Jack Straw's Castle in Hampstead where it was not unknown for Dickens to read the latest monthly instalments of his work to friends. John Foster, described Dickens's invitation to their first visit there together:

*'You don't feel disposed, do you, to muffle yourself up and start with me for a good brisk walk over Hampstead Heath? I know a good 'ouse there where we can have a red-hot chop for dinner, and a glass of good wine', leading to their 'first experience of Jack Straw's Castle, memorable for many happy meetings in coming years.'*

*Above: Tavistock House, Bloomsbury, London WC1 before it was demolished and below, the British Medical Association*
*Opposite page: Jack Straw's Castle, Hampstead, London NW3*

# Rules®

## LONDON'S OLDEST RESTAURANT

IN THE YEAR NAPOLEON OPENED HIS CAMPAIGN IN EGYPT, 1798, THOMAS RULE PROMISED HIS DESPAIRING FAMILY THAT HE WOULD SAY GOODBYE TO HIS WAYWARD PAST, SETTLE DOWN AND OPEN AN OYSTER BAR IN COVENT GARDEN.

RULES SERVES THE TRADITIONAL FOOD OF THIS COUNTRY AT ITS BEST — IT SPECIALISES IN CLASSIC GAME COOKERY AND IS FORTUNATE IN OWNING AN ESTATE IN THE HIGH PENNINES "ENGLAND'S LAST WILDERNESS" WHICH SUPPLIES GAME FOR THE RESTAURANT AND WHERE IT IS ABLE TO EXERCISE ITS OWN QUALITY CONTROLS AND DETERMINE HOW THE GAME IS TREATED.

THROUGHOUT ITS LONG HISTORY THE TABLES OF RULES HAVE BEEN CROWDED WITH WRITERS, ARTISTS, LAWYERS, JOURNALISTS AND ACTORS. AS WELL AS BEING FREQUENTED BY GREAT LITERARY TALENTS — CHARLES DICKENS, WILLIAM MAKEPEACE THACKERAY, JOHN GALSWORTHY & H G WELLS, RULES HAS ALSO APPEARED IN NOVELS BY ROSAMOND LEHMANN, EVELYN WAUGH, GRAHAM GREENE, JOHN LE CARRÉ, DICK FRANCIS AND CLAIRE RAYNER.

ON THE FIRST FLOOR, BY THE LATTICE WINDOW, WAS ONCE THE MOST CELEBRATED "TABLE FOR TWO" IN LONDON. THIS WAS THE PRINCE OF WALES' FAVOURITE SPOT FOR WINING AND DINING THE BEAUTIFUL ACTRESS LILLIE LANGTRY.

THE PAST LIVES ON AND IS CAPTURED IN LITERALLY HUNDREDS OF DRAWINGS, PAINTINGS AND CARTOONS. THE LATE JOHN BETJEMAN THEN POET LAUREATE DESCRIBED THE GROUND FLOOR INTERIOR AS "UNIQUE AND IRREPLACEABLE AND PART OF LITERARY AND THEATRICAL LONDON". IN ALL ITS 200 YEARS, SPANNING THE REIGNS OF NINE MONARCHS AND ENTERING ITS 4TH CENTURY IT HAS BEEN OWNED BY ONLY 3 FAMILIES.

# Bleak House

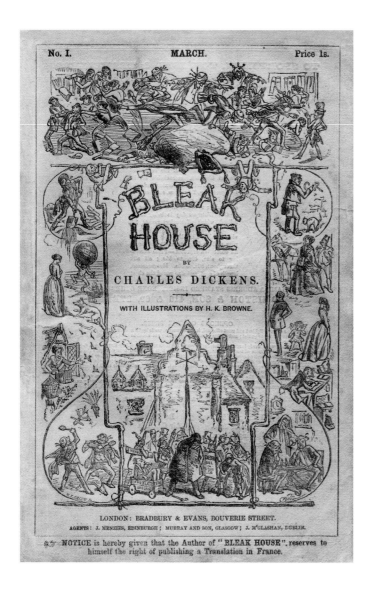

In April 1851, Dora, Dickens's infant daughter, died just a fortnight after his own father's death and she was buried in Highgate Cemetery, which would also one day be the last resting place of both his parents as well as Catherine, his wife.

Following Dora's death, Dickens set to work on *Bleak House* which appeared in monthly instalments between 1852-53 and, once again, Dickens incorporated places familiar to him.

At 26 Newman Street, Mr Turveydrop, *'a model of deportment'*, had his dance academy.

In *Bleak House*, Prince, the son of Mr Turveydrop, suggested to his father that he *'dine out comfortably, somewhere.'* *'My dear child, I intend to. I shall take my little meal, I think, at the French house, in the Opera Colonnade'*, replied his father.

This is now the Royal Opera Arcade which was designed by John Nash and G S Repton in 1816-18 and was Britain's original covered shopping arcade.

*Top left: Dora's grave, Highgate Cemetery*
*Left: Royal Opera Arcade, London SW1*
*Above: 26 Newman Strcc, London W1*

Staple Inn Buildings, dating from 1576, was one of the few to survive the fire of London. Dickens often mentioned how he liked the tranquillity of Staple Inn Square. Mr. Snagsby, in *Bleak House*, loved *'to walk in Staple Inn in the summertime and to observe how countrified the sparrows and leaves are'*. It also appeared in *Edwin Drood*.

*Above and Opposite page:*
*Staple Inn Square, London WC1. It was badly bombed during the Second World War and has been painstakingly recreated.*

Whilst writing *Bleak House*, according to Walter Dexter, one of the most diligent Dickensian historians, Charles Dickens spent a summer at Wylde's Farm in Hampstead. This claim cannot be verified from any other source. However all Dickens experts agree that Charles and Catherine stayed at the farm following Mary Hogarth's death.

Other famous occupants of the house over the years are William Blake and the painter John Linnell.

*Opposite page: The Law*
*Society, Chancery Lane*
*London WC2.*
*It was in Chancery Lane that*
*Old Tom Jarndyce blew his*
*brains out in despair*

*Above: Wylde's Farm,*
*Hampstead, London NW3*

Dickens was also known to have very strong views and experience of the supernatural. One such peculiar event happened just outside the Burlington Hotel, now an Art Gallery on the corner of Burlington Gardens.

Tired and *'used up'* after his usual wild hurry to finish the novel, Dickens related that:
*'I suddenly (the temperature being then most violent) found an icy coolness come upon me, accompanied with a general stagnation of the blood, a numbness of the extremities, great bewilderment of the mind, and a vague sensation of wonder. I was walking at the time, and, on looking round me, found that I was in the frigid shadow of the Burlington Hotel. Then I recollected that I had experienced the same sensations once before precisely in that spot. A curious case this, don't you think?'*

In the summer of 1855, Dickens and his family took up residence at number 3 Albion Villas, Folkestone - once again, overlooking the sea.

It was during this stay that he decided to give a public reading to assist in raising funds for a local institution. The reading, on 5th October 1855, was of *A Christmas Carol* and took place in the Folkestone Saw Mill, which Dickens described as *'a long carpenter's shop, as the biggest place that can be got.'* He insisted on a reduced admission price for working men – threepence (£0.75 today) as opposed to the standard price of five shillings (£15 today). Between 500 and 600 people attended.

*Opposite page:*
*The site of the*
*Burlington Hotel,*
*London W1*

*Above: 3 Albion Villas,*
*Folkestone, Kent*

*Following spread:*
*Folkestone, Kent*

# Public Performance

For the rest of his life, Dickens regularly conducted public readings. Rather than in theatres, these took place in public halls, assembly rooms and corn exchanges in towns and cities all across England, Wales, Scotland, Ireland and America. He also read at the British Embassy in Paris in January 1863.

Arguably the finest remaining example of these venues, to which Dickens was a regular visitor, is St. George's Hall in Liverpool, recently painstakingly restored by Liverpool City Council.

These readings were eagerly anticipated in much the same way a concert by a leading pop star would be today. They were exciting, hypnotic and always sold out. Some observers noted that it was as if he were possessed by some of his characters, such was the intensity and brilliance of his performance.

Dickens wrote to his sister-in-law of St George's Hall, *'The beautiful room was crammed to excess last night and numbers turned away. Its beauty and completeness when it is lighted up are most brilliant to behold, and for a reading it is simply perfect.'*

In 1866, he wrote to his daughter during a series of five readings from St George's Hall which he reported as his especial favourite, *'The police reported that three thousand people were turned away from the hall last night.'*

And on 15th February 1867, he wrote to his sister-in-law from Liverpool, *'We had an enormous turn-away last night, and do not doubt about having a cram to-night…The charming room here greatly lessens the fatigue of this fatiguing week.'*

At a banquet in his honour in Liverpool on 10th April 1869, Dickens stated: *'…Liverpool stood foremost among the great places out of London to which I had looked with eager confidence and pleasure…because it had been my happiness to have a public opportunity of testing the spirit of its people…all the response had been unsurpassable, spontaneous, open-handed, and munificent.'*

*Above and following spreads:*
*Exteriors and interiors of*
*St. George's Hall, Liverpool*

One of the few remaining theatres in which Dickens did actually perform was the Theatre Royal Haymarket where, in May 1848, he played Justice Shallow in eight performances of *The Merry Wives of Windsor* in order to help raise money to establish a curatorship at Shakespeare's birthplace in Stratford-upon-Avon. One of these performances was attended by Queen Victoria and Prince Albert.

What Dickens particularly enjoyed about the performing experience was that he felt it brought him into contact with his readers. His readings were a sell-out wherever he went; and although he wouldn't have people sitting behind him, he did talk about *'ladies sitting on the stairs.'* The wonderful thing for his readers was that these were the characters that they felt they knew personally. A lady once stopped him in the street and said, 'Mr. Dickens, let me touch the hand that has filled my home with so many friends.'

*Above and opposite page: Theatre Royal, Haymarket, London SW1*

# Good Works

Dickens banked with Coutts in the Strand, which still stands, although completely rebuilt since his day. It was then, as now, a private bank. Ironically, it is at the top of the same street where Warren's Blacking Factory once stood.

Amongst Coutts's own archive of cheques written by their more famous clients, they have four written by Charles Dickens.

Baroness Angela Burdett-Coutts, heiress to the banking fortune, was known as the 'Queen of the Poor' because of her many charitable causes. She and Dickens became firm friends and fellow campaigners in changing the plight of the poor and unfortunate.

*Left: Letters and cheques written by Charles Dickens from the Coutts archive*

*Opposite page: Two busts and a painting of Angela Burdett-Coutts on display at Coutts's bank, The Strand, London WC2*

Some of their many projects included the establishment of 'Urania Cottage' in Lime Grove, Shepherd's Bush, as a 'Home for Homeless Women'. This was intended for the rehabilitation of 'women on the streets', a Victorian euphemism for prostitutes. This opened in 1847 at a time when Shepherd's Bush was still farming land outside of London.

With the sprawl of urbanisation in the late 1800 and early 1900's, the site next door eventually became Gainsborough Film Studios, and then, BBC Lime Grove Studios, where a number of the BBC's early television adaptations of Dickens's works were recorded.

The name of the cottage, 'Urania', had been established by a previous owner but was particularly unsuitable in this instance, as Aphrodite Urania or Celestial Aphrodite is the goddess of pure and spiritual love.

Dickens and Angela also worked on helping to support the 'Field Lane Ragged School', which was part of a charitable education concept designed to provide free schooling, clothes and lodging to poor or 'ragged' children.

*Top left: Urania Cottage, Lime Grove, London W12*
*Bottom left: The site today*

# Little Dorrit

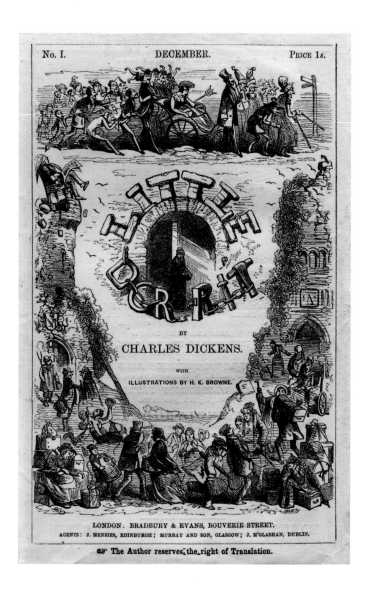

With his characteristic restlessness, after further trips to Paris, Dickens threw himself into his next novel. Between 1855 and 1857, *Little Dorrit* appeared in monthly instalments.

He used The George Inn in The Borough, the only remaining galleried inn in London, as the location where Edward Dorrit wrote a begging letter to Arthur Clennam.

*"And if Mr Tip--if he happens to be a coming in as I come out, and if he says "Where are you going, Maggy?" and if I says, "I'm a going So and So," and if he says, "I'll have a Try too," and if he goes into the George and writes a letter and if he gives it me and says, "Take that one to the same place, and if the answer's a good 'un I'll give you a shilling," it ain't my fault, mother!'*

*Opposite page: The George Inn, The Borough, London SE1*

Dickens's scorn for certain aspects of Government is probably best highlighted in his depiction of the fictitious Circumlocution Office in *Little Dorrit*:

*'If another Gunpowder Plot had been discovered half an hour before the lighting of the match, nobody would have been justified in saving the parliament until there had been half a score of boards, half a bushel of minutes, several sacks of official memoranda, and a family-vault full of ungrammatical correspondence, on the part of the Circumlocution Office.'*

Not surprisingly no current Government department we contacted would lay claim to being the inspiration for the Circumlocution Office.

*Opposite page:*
*Top: Borough Market, London SE1*
*Bottom: Derek Jacobi as Arthur Clennam,*
*in the feature film of* Little Dorrit

*Above: St Bart's Hospital, London EC1,*
*was where John Baptist Cavalletto was*
*taken after being hit by the mail coach*

*Left: Amy Dorrit or 'Little Dorrit' loved to walk on Southwark Bridge. Indeed, John Chivery proposed to her on Southwark Bridge, London SE1, although the bridge of Dickens's time was replaced in 1912 with this one*

The Church of St George the Martyr in The Borough is where Amy Dorrit is christened and later married to Arthur Clennam. Every year, a service organised by The International Dickens Fellowship takes place in the church in May.

*Above: Amy Dorrit also spends the night in the church one night after being locked out of The Marshalsea. On the day we photographed the church, it looked as if someone else had spent the previous night there*

*Left: Amy Dorrit in the stained glass window in the church of St. George the Martyr, London SE1*

191

# Gad's Hill

Enjoying such sustained success, Dickens could now turn his attention to fulfilling his childhood dream of purchasing the house that he and his father had passed so often on their walks, Gad's Hill Place.

Dickens, ever the keen man of business, initially offered £1,500 for the house but this was rejected. He finally bought it for £1,790 (£105,000 today) on Friday 14th March 1856.

He had actually used the house in *A Christmas Carol*. The ghost of Christmas Past takes Scrooge back to his boy-hood and his old school - *'a mansion of dull red brick with a little weathercock-surmounted cupola, on the roof, and a bell hanging in it.'*

Dickens spent a great deal of time and money improving the property but was not to move into it, on a full time basis, until 1860.

*Left and opposite: Gad's Hill, Kent*

## GADS HILL PLACE

"Ever since I can recollect, my father,
seeing me so fond of it, has often said to me,
"If you were to be very persevering and were to
work hard, you might some day come to live in it."

CHARLES DICKENS fulfilled his father's prophecy
when he acquired it in 1856. It was then his home
until he died here on 9th June, 1870

PRESENTED BY THE STROOD RURAL DISTRICT
COUNCIL                                    MAY 1969

This is the Grave of DICK The Best of Birds Born — at Broadstairs Mid 1851 Died at Gads Hill Place 14th Oct. 1866

# CHRISTMAS SPORTS,

AT

## Mr. Charles Dickens's Cricket Field,

# ON BOXING DAY, 1866,

To Commence at Half-past Ten to the Moment.

Open to Members of the Gadshill, Higham, Chalk, and Shorne Cricket Clubs. Entries to be made, free of all charge, with Mr. Russell, before One o'clock on Wednesday, December 19th, when the Lists will be finally closed. Colours will be distributed on the Ground.

THE FOLLOWING RACES

This move to North Kent was a return to the idyll of his countryside childhood in nearby Chatham. He made several changes there, many of which still survive, such as the false bookshelf on the inside of the study door. The books, all fictitious have humourous titles such as *'Hansards Guide to Refreshing Sleep', 'Lady Godiva and her Horse', 'Cats Lives - in nine volumes'* and *'History of a Short Chancery Suit'* - in nineteen volumes.

He also converted a bedroom into a library and constructed a conservatory, which he would first see completed on Sunday, 5th June, just four days before his death.

Dickens loved to entertain the local villagers in the grounds, arranging cricket matches and running races.

The house is now a school and two of Dickens's great-great-grandaughters would later be educated there.

Dickens's old study is now occupied by the headmaster.

*Above: The public house just
opposite Gad's Hill Place, the Sir
John Falstaff Inn, was the local in
which Dickens drank or from which
he had drink sent over. The landlord
there also acted as a banker for him,
regularly cashing his cheques*

*Right: The tunnel joined Gad's Hill
to Dickens's writing chalet*

*Opposite page: Charles Dickens and
his daughters, Kate and Mamie*

Dickens loved to write in his chalet, one of his most treasured possessions and a gift from his actor friend, Charles Fechter. It was erected in the garden at Gad's Hill Place, on the other side of the busy road in front of the house. In order to reach it in safety, a tunnel was constructed under the supervision of Alfred Dickens and Henry Austin so that Dickens would not have to worry about being struck by a cart whilst his mind worked out his plot lines as he walked. Today, the Chalet stands in the grounds of Eastgate House in Rochester High Street.

*Left: Paul Horton, caretaker of Eastgate House and the Chalet*
*Following spread: Ellen Ternan and the All The Year Round office current tenants, Dr Jonathan Freeman and family*

In the late 1850s, although only in his forties, Dickens looked lined and exhausted. He worked extremely hard and it showed in his face. Gone was the handsome young man, prematurely worn-out with writing novels, running magazines, supporting his family and generally being one of the great public figures of the day. He was also now deeply unhappy in his marriage to the aging, lethargic and, frankly, unloved Catherine.

Although his family was a constant drain upon him, Dickens was now a considerably rich man. If other successful men might have been tempted to take life at a much easier pace, not Charles Dickens; he continued to drive himself ever harder. As well as his stories, there was still journalism and his entrepreneurial ventures in publishing and editing, not to mention his much loved performing.

He threw himself into some sophisticated amateur theatricals where all the theatricality of his fiction could now be given full rein. And it was while involved in one of these, in 1857, that he met Ellen Ternan, aged eighteen, nearly the same age as Dickens's daughter, Kate.

Dickens was absorbed in a Wilkie Collins play, *The Frozen Deep*, which he partially re-wrote and produced and in which he played the lead role of Richard Wardour. There was a private performance for the Queen, Prince Albert and the King of Belgium. On tour, the cast was joined by Maria and Ellen Ternan, who were specifically engaged for the performance at the Free Trade Hall in Manchester. Rumours of an affair between Dickens and Ellen culminated in his separation from Catherine in 1858. Divorce was out of the question, but Dickens and Catherine now embarked upon living apart. He remained at Gad's Hill.

His daughters, Kate and Mamie, stood high in their father's eye, but his sons less so. One exception was Henry Fielding Dickens, a distinguished lawyer who became Common Serjeant of England, one of the highest law officers of the land. He died in 1933.

In 1859, whilst working to dissolve his *Household Words* journal, with premises at 16 Wellington Street, Dickens was already determined to start its successor, which he called *All The Year Round*. This ran from 1859 to 1870, under Dickens's editorship, and continued afterwards under his son, Charley, until the 1890s.

This publication had offices in 11 Wellington Street, also providing Dickens with lodgings in London above his editorial premises for a few years in the late 1860s before he died. He would stay here when conducting his London readings. His fireplace is all that remains of the interior.

*All The Year Round* became very popular and was eagerly anticipated by readers. The first issue of this new journal contained the opening instalment of a new novel he had been working on, *A Tale Of Two Cites*.

# A Tale Of Two Cities

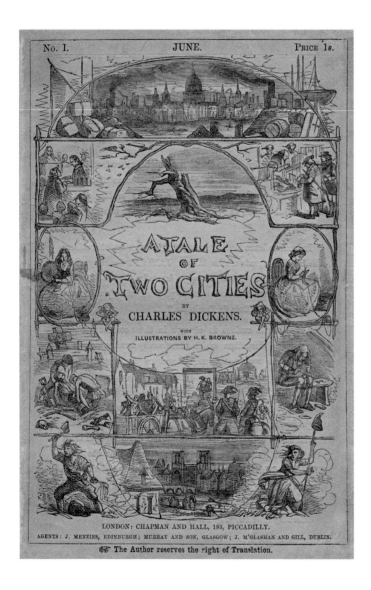

*A Tale Of Two Cities* is one the few Dickens stories that takes place partly abroad. With much of the action set in France, he once again interweaves known locations within the story.

The lodgings of Dr Manette were located in a quiet street corner, not far from Soho Square.

'*A quainter corner than the corner where the Doctor lived, was not to be found in London. There was no way through it, and the front windows of the Doctor's lodgings commanded a pleasant little vista of street that had a congenial air of retirement on it. There were few buildings then, north of the Oxford-road, and forest-trees flourished, and wild flowers grew, and the hawthorn blossomed, in the now vanished fields.*'...

*... "In a building at the back, attainable by a court-yard' where a plane-tree rustled its green leaves, church-organs claimed to be made, and silver to be chased, and likewise gold to be beaten by some mysterious giant who had a golden arm starting out of the wall of the front hall--as if he had beaten himself precious, and menaced a similar conversion of all visitors."*

*Above and left: Manette Street in Soho, London W1, was Rose Street in Dickens's time however in 1895 it adopted its current name in honour of Dickens. A replica of the Goldbeaters Arm can still be seen in the street at the side of Foyle's bookstore. The original, used by Dickens in the story is in The Charles Dickens Museum*

*A Tale of Two Cities* also cites the incident where *'that magnificent potentate, the Lord Mayor of London, was made to stand and deliver on Turnham Green, by one highwayman, who despoiled the illustrious creature in sight of all his retinue.'*

These days, a Lord Mayor of London is more likely to live in this desirable part of London rather than be robbed in it. Although Turnham Green itself remains, it is, today, much reduced in size, mainly serving as a park for dog walking.

Charles Darney was tried for treason at the Old Bailey, but was acquitted because of his close resemblance to Sydney Carton.

The Old Bailey, much rebuilt, now covers the site of Newgate Prison, the gaol where Fagin spent his last hours before being hanged in its courtyard. Newgate Prison was also frequently used by Dickens in *Nicholas Nickleby, The Old Curiosity Shop* and *Barnaby Rudge*. In *Great Expectations*, Pip was taken inside by Mr. Jaggers's clerk, Wemmick:
*'It was visiting time when Wemmick took me in; and a pot man was going his rounds with beer; and the prisoners, behind bars in yards, were buying beer, and talking to friends; and a frousy, ugly, disorderly, depressing scene it was.'*

The lawyer, Mr Stryver, has chambers within the Temple where his clerk, Sydney Carton, *'turned into the Temple, and, having revived himself by twice pacing the pavements of King's Bench-walk and Paper-buildings, turned into the Stryver chambers.'*

*Top left: Turnham Green, Chiswick London W4*
*Middle left: The Old Bailey, London WC2*
*Bottom left: Kings Bench Walk,*
*The Temple, London WC2*

By 1860, disenchanted with Tavistock House because of its unpleasant memories and suffering from rheumatism in his left side as well as neuralgia of the face, both harbingers of serious ill-health which he chose to ignore, Dickens's plans were interrupted by the sudden death of his brother, Alfred.

He immediately brought his brother's family to a cottage near Gad's Hill Place while he sought a London accommodation for them. It was in this transitional atmosphere that he launched into his next masterpiece, *Great Expectations*, which appeared in weekly instalments in 1860-61.

*On the 4th September, 1860 Dickens wrote:*
*'Yesterday I burnt, in the field at Gad's Hill,*
*the accumulated letters and papers of twenty*
*years. They set up a smoke like the genie*
*when he got out of the casket on the seashore;*
*and as it was an exquisite day when I began,*
*and rained very heavily when I finished,*
*I suspect my correspondence of having*
*overcast the face of the heavens'*

In *The Uncommercial Traveller*, also published in 1861, Dickens made much of the churchyard at St. Olave's:

*'One of my best beloved churchyards, I call the churchyard of Saint Ghastly Grim; touching what men in general call it, I have no information. It lies at the heart of the City, and the Blackwall Railway shrieks at it daily. It is a small small churchyard, with a ferocious, strong, spiked iron gate, like a jail. This gate is ornamented with skulls and cross-bones, larger than the life, wrought in stone; but it likewise came into the mind of Saint Ghastly Grim, that to stick iron spikes a-top of the stone skulls, as though they were impaled, would be a pleasant device. Therefore the skulls grin aloft horribly, thrust through and through with iron spears. Hence, there is attraction of repulsion for me in Saint Ghastly Grim, and, having often contemplated it in the daylight and the dark, I once felt drawn towards it in a thunderstorm at midnight. 'Why not?' I said, in self-excuse. 'I have been to see the Colosseum by the light of the moon; is it worse to go to see Saint Ghastly Grim by the light of the lightning?' I repaired to the Saint in a hackney cab, and found the skulls most effective, having the air of a public execution, and seeming, as the lightning flashed, to wink and grin with the pain of the spikes. Having no other person to whom to impart my satisfaction, I communicated it to the driver. So far from being responsive, he surveyed me--he was naturally a bottled-nosed, red-faced man--with a blanched countenance. And as he drove me back, he ever and again glanced in over his shoulder through the little front window of his carriage, as mistrusting that I was a fare originally from a grave in the churchyard of Saint Ghastly Grim, who might have flitted home again without paying.'*

# Great Expectations

In *Great Expectations*, the family home of Herbert Pocket is in Hammersmith by the river. Estella completes her education in Hammersmith.

*"....we went back to Barnard's Inn and got my little portmanteau, and then took coach for Hammersmith. We arrived there at two or three o'clock in the afternoon, and had very little way to walk to Mr. Pocket's house. Lifting the latch of a gate, we passed direct into a little garden overlooking the river, where Mr. Pocket's children were playing about. And unless I deceive myself on a point where my interests or prepossessions are certainly not concerned, I saw that Mr. and Mrs. Pocket's children were not growing up or being brought up, but were tumbling up. Mrs. Pocket was sitting on a garden chair under a tree, reading, with her legs upon another garden chair; and Mrs. Pocket's two nursemaids were looking about them while the children played. "Mamma," said Herbert, "this is young Mr. Pip." Upon which Mrs. Pocket received me with an appearance of amiable dignity."*

*Opposite page: Hammersmith, London W6*

*'Joe's forge adjoined our house, which was a wooden house, as many of the dwellings in our country were - most of them, at that time.'*

*Opposite page: This Old Forge in Chalk, Kent, is believed to be the inspiration for Joe Gargery's forge in Great Expectations*

*Above: This building features as Uncle Pumblechook's corn-chandler's business and house in Great Expectations and again, in The Mystery of Edwin Drood, as the offices of Mr. Sapsea, an auctioneer*

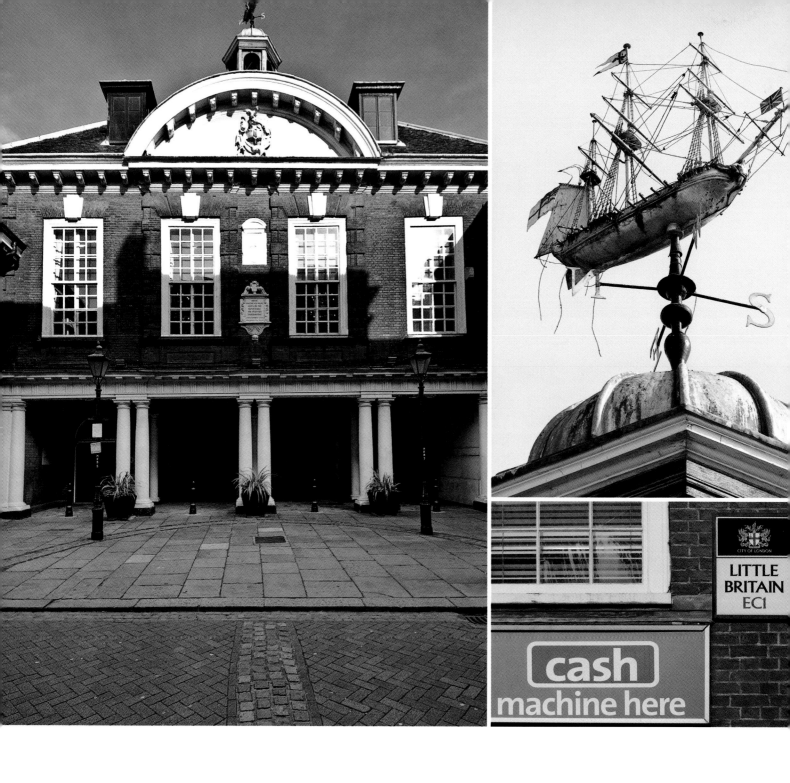

*Above and top right: The Guildhall, Rochester, Kent, featured as the court where Pip was brought by Mr. Pumblechook to be bound over as an apprentice to Joe Gargery.*
*Right bottom: Mr Jaggers who is employed by both Miss Havisham and by Abel Magwitch has his office in Little Britain. It is here that Pip finds out the truth about Estella's past when Jaggers puts the "imaginary case" to him*

*Above: Little Britain, London EC1*

*Opposite page: Rochester Bridge, Kent*

CITY OF ROCHESTER

RESTORATION HOUSE

BUILT IN 1587 IT IS SAID THAT CHARLES II
STAYED HERE ON THE NIGHT OF 28TH MAY 1660
AT HIS RESTORATION. THE SATIS HOUSE OF
GREAT EXPECTATIONS"

RESTORATION
HOUSE & GARDEN
OPEN JUNE TO SEPT
10 AM TO 5 PM
THUR & FRI

There are often very close parallels between the real women in Dickens's life and his fictional characters. We know that he was very fond of his elder sister, Fanny, who was a singer, they were very close as children; and also, of course, his mother. He is supposed to have described her as Mrs. Nickleby, the muddleheaded character who is, of course, a great rattle. In one of the prefaces to Nicholas Nickleby, he said that Mrs. Nickleby herself says 'did I ever suppose there could be such a woman?'

But Estella in Great Expectations, was, of course, more likely to have been based on his first unhappy love affair with Maria Beadnell. Some people have speculated that perhaps it might be Ellen Ternan because he was becoming involved with her at the time he was writing the novel. But there is just no way that such a young woman, so over-awed by this famous man, would have treated him in the heartless way that Estella treats Pip. In fact, Dickens referred to Ellen as 'the charmer' in a letter; hardly a description that would apply to Estella.

The amazing thing is that we don't think Dickens used his dear wife, Catherine, at all in his fiction; although some people have suggested that perhaps she's Agnes Wickfield in David Copperfield, the wonderful 'legless' heroine of Victorian fiction, as somebody called her. Perhaps this is so because it's very difficult to write about good people; it's much more exciting to write about the grotesques and the terrible people. But certainly we think that some of the later, lively young girls, such as Bella Wilfer in Our Mutual Friend and Rosa Budd in The Mystery of Edwin Drood, could be reflections of Ellen Ternan or perhaps even his daughter, Kate. Occasionally, some of the people who Dickens modelled his characters on recognised themselves and complained. A famous example was that of the dwarf manicurist, Miss Mowcher in David Copperfield.

Her character was based on Mrs Jane Seymour Hill, a manicurist and chiropodist, of 6 York Gate, Regent's Park, a near-neighbour of Charles Dickens. A dwarf, she was greatly distressed by what she and others were convinced was the portrait of her as Miss Mowcher, introduced into the December monthly edition of David Copperfield (Ch. 22).

Mrs Hill had written to Dickens on 18th December: 'I have suffered long and much from my personal deformities but never before at the hands of a Man so highly gifted as Charles Dickens and hitherto considered as a Christian and Friend to his fellow Creatures.'

Because it was very unkind, Dickens was very contrite. When Miss Mowcher comes into the story later on, she is far more sympathetically treated. The character puts the case for the difficulties of the physical misfortune that afflicts her and all the members of her family. It's quite a plea. 'If I am a plaything for you giants, be gentle with me.'

There have been many speculative attempts to determine the model for Miss Havisham in Great Expectations. At one time, one was said to be an Australian woman, Eliza Donnithorne, described as 'Sydney's Miss Havisham', who, in fact, could not possibly have come to Dickens's attention until several years after the novel was published. The character of Miss Havisham is much more likely to have been based on a woman Dickens wrote about in an essay, Where We Stopped Growing: The White Woman of Berners Street.

That was a woman who had been jilted by a Quaker; and she went about simpering in her white wedding dress. Dickens said he thought that Quaker had had a lucky escape.

**THELMA GROVE**
**Honorary Life Member, The International Dickens Fellowship**

# Cooling

St. James's Church Cooling, stands a few miles from Rochester and right on the edge of the marshes and it has changed little since Dickens's time.

In the opening chapter of *Great Expectations*, Magwitch has just escaped from one of the prison hulks on the estuary just a short distance away. Dickens describes Pip standing over a grave with *'five little stone lozenges, each a foot and a half long'*, representing the graves of his five brothers.

In the churchyard there are actually thirteen childrens' graves, all belonging to just two families, the Comports and the Bakers, whose children had died from marsh-fever.

And Dickens's choice of the name, 'Magwitch', is interesting. It's a variation on 'Madgewick', an old Portsmouth name. Dickens liked to find a use for all manner of stored up information, eventually.

*Above and opposite page: St James Church, Cooling, Kent*

'Hold your noise!' cried a terrible voice, as a man started up from among the graves at the side of the church porch. 'Keep still, you little devil, or I'll cut your throat!'

A fearful man, all in course grey, with a great iron on his leg. A man with no hat, and with broken shoes, and with an old rag tied round his head. A man who had been soaked in water, and smothered in mud, and lamed by stones, and cut by flints, and stung by nettles, and torn by briars; who limped, and shivered, and glared and growled; and whose teeth chattered in his head as he seized me by the chin.

'O! Don't cut my throat, sir,' I pleaded in terror. 'Pray don't do it, sir.'

'Tell us your name!' said the man. 'Quick!'

'Pip, sir.'

'Once More,' said the man, staring at me. 'Give it mouth!'

'Pip. Pip, sir.'

**Great Expectations**

# Our Mutual Friend

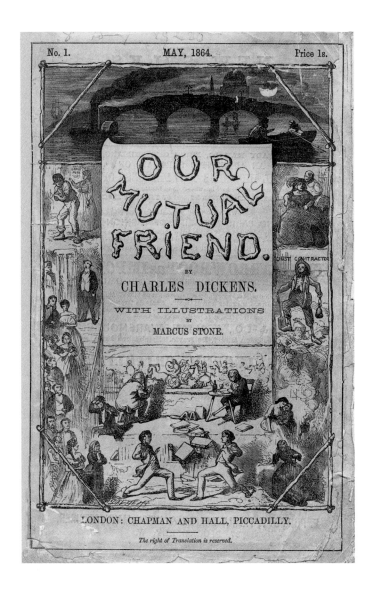

In 1863, Dickens dwelt amidst an atmosphere permeated by death – his mother-in-law, Mrs. Hogarth, died, followed by the death of his own mother on 13th September; and after a curious and unexplained premonition of a funeral, he would also learn the following February that his son, Walter, had also fallen dead in Calcutta.

After more than two years attempting to write, Dickens began work on *Our Mutual Friend* which appeared in monthly parts between 1864-65.

The River Thames is London's main artery; and so it is, in some ways, also for Charles Dickens and his stories.

The grotesque dwarf Quilp, in *The Old Curiosity Shop*, is drowned, with the water playing with his corpse, dragging it through the mud and the long grass and finally dumping it onto a swamp to rot and fester. In *Our Mutual Friend*, all the misery, poverty and corruption stems from the London riverside, an illustration perhaps of the misery Dickens felt when he worked by the Thames at Warren's Blacking Factory.

Drawing upon his childhood visits to his godfather's house nearby, now, so many years later, Dickens drew upon the nearby Grapes Public House in Narrow Street, Limehouse which he re-christened 'The Six Jolly Fellowship Porters' for *Our Mutual Friend*.

'*In its whole constitution it had not a straight floor, and hardly a straight line; but it had outlasted, and clearly would yet outlast, many a better-trimmed building, many a sprucer public-house.*'

*Top left: Landlady Barbara Hague. The Grapes public house, Limehouse, City of London, has outlasted a great many of the public houses in this area*

*'The abode of Mrs Betty Higden was not easy to find, lying in such complicated back settlements of muddy Brentford.'*

Mrs. Betty Higden, who, in *Our Mutual Friend*, is so insistent that she does not want to end up in the workhouse, lived by the river. Although Brentford today remains just as muddy at low tide, these days the only people who can afford to live by the river Thames occupy an entirely opposite social standing.

The river is the central point of focus in *Our Mutual Friend*, following its journey inland and its affect on the story's assorted characters. As well as London, Henley-on-Thames, home of the world-renowned Regatta, is featured. The Angler's Inn, where Eugene Wrayburn stayed and was nursed by Lizzie Hexam before the couple's eventual wedding there, is based on the Red Lion Inn in Henley-on-Thames.

*Opposite page, top left: Exclusive pent house apartments overlooking the River Thames at Brentford, Middlesex*

*Right: The Red Lion Hotel, Henley-on-Thames, Oxforshire*

# Staplehurst

In 1865, as well as continuing his reading tours, Dickens seemed to have been crossing the channel 'perpetually' because his visits to Condette, near Boulogne, helped to soothe the neuralgia from which he was now constantly suffering. This was only one of a number of serious health concerns afflicting him by now, which he stoically attempted to rise above. It was also possibly to see Ellen Ternan. It is felt that he may have persuaded her to live in France as any discovery of their relationship there was far less likely to have an adverse effect.

On the 9th June 1865, Dickens was returning from France via the Boulogne to Folkestone ferry with Ellen Ternan and her mother. They boarded the 2:38pm tidal train from Folkestone Harbour Station and were seated in a First Class carriage. At around 3:10pm, they were approaching the River Beult, just outside of Staplehurst in Kent. Unknown to everyone aboard, however, they were travelling at fifty miles per hour towards repair work which was being carried out on the very small viaduct which then stood where today's bridge now stands - and the rails had been removed. The foreman in charge of the work had consulted the wrong time-table and, so, was not expecting the tidal train for another two hours.

*Right: Entrance and track to the old Folkestone Harbour Station, Kent*

*Opposite page: The site of the Staplehurst, Kent, train crash today*

The flagman, who was supposed to give warning to any oncoming trains was only five hundred and fifty yards from the construction site. And in order to have had any positive effect, he would have to have been much further down the line.

Although the engine driver saw the red flag and even applied his brakes, the stopping time was not enough and all the first class carriages plummeted into the gaping void down into the river below: all, that is, except the one that Dickens and his party were in. Dickens's carriage was saved solely by the weight of the second class carriages behind that left it dangling precariously over the edge of the bridge

Dickens, aged fifty-three, managed to clamber out and help his companions to safety. He then began helping other injured people. In a letter to a friend, Thomas Mitton, on 13th June 1865, Dickens wrote:

*'I am a little shaken, not by the beating and dragging of the carriage in which I was, but by the hard work afterwards in getting out the dying and dead, which was most horrible*

*Suddenly I came upon a staggering man covered with blood (I think he must have been flung clean out of his carriage) with such a frightful cut across the skull that I couldn't bear to look at him. I poured some water over his face, and gave him some to drink, and gave him some brandy, and laid him down on the grass, and he said, "I am gone", and died afterwards. Then I stumbled over a lady lying on her back against a little pollard tree, with the blood streaming over her face (which was lead colour) in a number of distinct little streams from the head. I asked her if she could swallow a little brandy, and she just nodded, and I gave her some and left her for somebody else. The next time I passed her, she was dead.'*

One passenger reported how Dickens, with his hat full of water, was *'running about with it and doing his best to revive and comfort every poor creature he met who had sustained serious injury.'*

Then, as he was about to leave, Dickens remembered that the manuscript for the latest instalment of what would prove to be his last completed novel, *Our Mutual Friend*, was still inside the pocket of his overcoat, which hung within the precarious carriage that teetered above the river. He climbed back inside in order to retrieve it. Only then, did he travel on to London with the other survivors on an emergency train.

Thereafter, Dickens never looked upon train journeys without a sense of anxiety. There were more train crashes in the 1860s than any other decade in British travel history. Nevertheless, having a celebrated novelist so closely caught up in such a catastrophe served to raise both the public's and the authorities' awareness of the risks attached to this growing mode of transport, helping to concentrate their minds more effectively on safety concerns.

*Above: This picture of the Staplehurst rail crash was taken several days after the tragic accident by a Broadstairs photographer. His grandaughter donated it to the Dickens House Museum Broadstairs and this is the first time it has been published in a book*

*Opposite page: From the front page of the Illustrated London News*

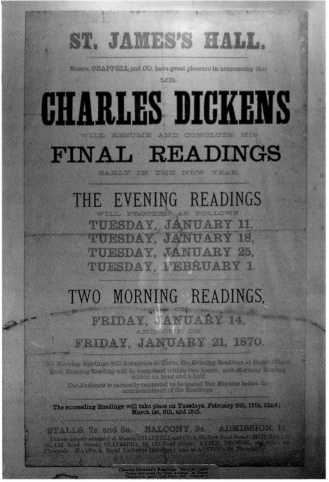

In 1868, despite numerous warnings of potential health problems, Dickens undertook another gruelling tour of America. Although this earned £20,000 after expenses (worth £920,000 today), it cost him dearly in its adverse effects upon his declining physical condition. He literally limped out of America, exhausted and ill, but recuperated on the journey home.

That autumn, he incorporated an impassioned reading of Nancy's murder from *Oliver Twist* which sapped his energy to such an extent that he collapsed twice, insisting however on finishing the readings. His doctors eventually forced him to rest when he showed early signs of paralysis in his left side.

*Top left: This leather bag was used on Charles Dickens's first reading tour by his manager, Arthur Smith, who had to collect all his takings and carry them about in the bag. Dickens wrote in his letters, 'Poor Arthur Smith has got forty shillings of silver which must be very uncomfortable for him to sit on'*

*Left: Tony White, current owner of The Leather Bottle Cobham, found this poster discarded behind a chest of drawers*

# The Mystery of Edwin Drood

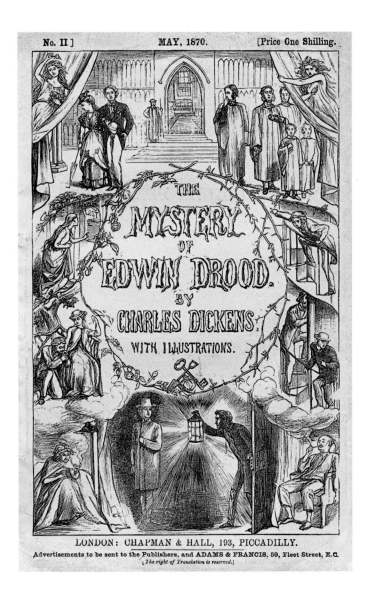

No. II ]      MAY, 1870.      [Price One Shilling.

THE MYSTERY OF EDWIN DROOD. BY CHARLES DICKENS. WITH ILLUSTRATIONS.

LONDON: CHAPMAN & HALL, 193, PICCADILLY.

Advertisements to be sent to the Publishers, and ADAMS & FRANCIS, 59, Fleet Street, E.C.

[ The right of Translation is reserved.]

In 1870, Dickens began work on his final novel, *The Mystery of Edwin Drood*. At Minor Canon Row, Dickens likened the front porches to *'sounding boards over old pulpits.'*

Dickens described Jasper's Gatehouse & Mr. Tope's House as if they were one, linked by a connecting door.

The Vines featured in the book as the Monk's Vineyard. Dickens himself was seen leaning against a fence here just two days before he died.

*Opposite page, top: Mr Tope's House and Jasper's Gatehouse, Rochester, Kent*
*Bottom: Minor Canon Row, Rochester*

*Following spread: The Vines, Rochester. It would also have served as the presumed route Pip would have taken to visit Miss Havisham*

**THE MONK**

# The Final Chapter

Even Rochester Castle, which Dickens knew well from his childhood, reminded him of his own mortality. In *Household Words* he observed, *'I surveyed the massive ruin from the Bridge, and thought what a brief little practical joke I seemed to be, in comparison with its solidity, stature, strength and length of life.'*

After organising some theatricals for friends, Dickens returned to Gad's Hill Place on 3rd June to resume work on *The Mystery of Edwin Drood*. Only six parts were ever published.

Although by now he was very ill he did not complain to anyone although most people who observed him commented on how exhausted he looked.

On Tuesday 7th June he drove to Cobham Wood with his sister-in-law and walked round the park and wood making his way back to Gad's Hill. He returned in time to put up, in his new conservatory, some Chinese lanterns that had arrived from London that afternoon.

*Left and opposite page: Rochester Castle*

On 8th June, after working all day in the chalet of his garden, he was dining with Georgina Hogarth, when he collapsed at 6pm. The following evening, 9th June 1870, at 6:10pm, he died of a brain haemorrhage.

He was fifty-eight years old and had endeavoured to fill every moment of his life. Leaving a total estate valued at £93,000 (over £ 4 million today) his bequest to mankind was far, far in excess of this.

*Previous Spread: Cobham Woods, Kent*

Having been inspired for the whole of his professional career by Rochester, his description in *The Mystery of Edwin Drood* from some of the very last paragraphs he wrote is particularly poignant:

'*A brilliant morning shines on the old city. Its antiquities and ruins are surpassingly beautiful, with a lusty ivy gleaming in the sun, and the rich trees waving in the balmy air. Changes of glorious light from moving boughs, songs of birds, scents from gardens, woods, and fields –*'

*Opposite page: The dining room at Gad's Hill Place, taken around the time of Dickens's death*

*Above: His grave in Poets' Corner was left open for several days, so great was the constant procession of people from all walks of life who came to pay their respects and bid their final farewells, until the grave itself disappeared under the mound of floral tributes. At last, 'Boz' could rest. Although it is said, his ghost continues to haunt the moat at Rochester Castle*

*Left: The Vines, Rochester 'a glorious light from moving boughs'*

GEORGE FREDERICK HANDEL Esq.
born February XXIII. MDCLXXXIV.
died April XIV. MDCCLIX.    L.F.Roubiliac invt et sct

GEORGE FREDERIC HANDEL
BORN Y 23 FEBRUARY 1684
DIED Y 14th OF APRIL 1759·

CHARLES DICKENS
BORN 7TH FEBRUARY 1812
DIED 9TH JUNE 1870

RUDYA

BORN

DIE

Though he had stipulated his wish to be buried quietly in Rochester, without pomp and ceremony - several locations were suggested, including Cobham and Shorne churches and Rochester Castle moat, nevertheless, various members of the establishment demanded he be buried here in Westminster Abbey.

His family agreed, providing that the funeral adhere to the terms dictated in his will: that it be quiet, private, unadvertised and unostentatious and that his name be carved very plainly.

The admission cards for the memorial service in Westminster Abbey contained his response to the audience following his final public reading. Moved to tears by the tumultuous applause he had received, with great difficulty, he delivered his parting words: *'From these garish lights I vanish now for evermore with a heartfelt, grateful, respectful, affectionate farewell.'*

*This and following spread:*
*Westminster Abbey, London SW1*

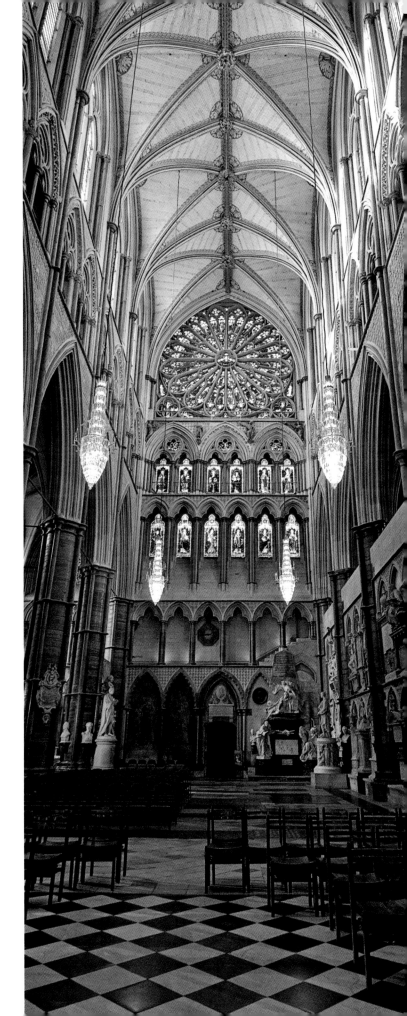

*Previous spread: Dickens had suggested that Shorne churchyard, Kent, would be a fitting place to be buried*

*Above: John Forster states that when Dickens died he should like to lie in the little graveyard at the foot of Rochester Castle wall*

*Left: In a gesture that could have come from the pages of one of his stories, his daughter Kate donated the couch on which Charles Dickens died to the Birthplace Museum in Portsmouth so that the places of his birth and death might be united*

*Opposite page: Highland Cemetery, Portsmouth*

One of the criticisms levelled against Dickens - by Virginia Woolf and Henry James amongst others   was the number of outlandish coincidences that occur in his stories:  In *Oliver Twist*, the Artful Dodger and Charlie Bates pick the pocket of the man who turns out to be Oliver Twist's grandfather, Mr Brownlow; in *A Tale Of Two Cities*, Sydney Carton and Charles Darnay have a physical resemblance that deceives many; in *Great Expectations*, Estella turns out to be the daughter of Abel Magwitch. However, in reality, the death of Dickens and some of those he knew threw up coincidences far more unbelievable than any he wrote about.

Dickens died exactly five years to the day of the Staplehurst rail crash.

In another strangely Dickensian twist, Dickens's first love, Maria Beadnell, and his last love, Ellen Ternan, are both unaccountably buried in the same cemetery in Portsmouth, the town of his birth. For completely unrelated reasons, both women ended up living there. They did not know each other and it is unlikely that either knew of the other's relationship with Charles Dickens. Even though there are four cemeteries in the city, they or their loved ones chose the Highland Road Cemetery, and their graves are also quite near each other. Dickens would have relished this coincidence.

# What the Dickens?

This is the end of our journey through CHARLES DICKENS'S ENGLAND. It can, of course, only touch upon the surface of the country he loved so much, understood so well and explored so thoroughly, as the backdrop for all his stories. Although so much in England, and particularly London, has changed in the one and a half centuries since his death, it is nonetheless surprising how much still remains. Gone are the workhouses, the cruel educational establishments, the debtors prisons, the no-go areas of Seven Dials, the child labour factories, the seven day working week - gone thanks, in no small part, to Charles Dickens, who highlighted the plight of the poor and dispossessed, the forgotten and bullied, the weak and the unfortunate. Through the astonishing range of characters and conditions that sprang from his penetrating observations, he gave a voice to the thousands of actual people who would be beneficially served by them, far more effectively than any charitable, religious or government institution could possibly have done.

If Charles Dickens's England has gone, his literary legacy remains unchallenged, and will continue to thrive for generations to come. Thanks to the latest available technologies such as the internet, his body of work is now freely available for future audiences to discover the glorious genius from a man whose stories will never age.

Through them, we can glimpse not just the bad things he observed throughout his lifetime, but also the good things, seen through the eyes of the colourful characters he introduced along the way, drawn either from life itself or created by his exceptional and unrivalled imagination.

THE
CHARLES DICKENS

FIREWORKS
EVERY WEDNESDAY
OVER VIKING BAY
Starting Wednesday
30th July

Fine Wines
& ALES

Welcome to
THE
CHARLES
DICKENS

Real Ale & Good
FOOD

★ ALBION STREET

barnaby rudge

1926

Live MUSIC every MONDAY From 8·30 Nite...

The Old Curiosity Shop
Tea Rooms

SALMON
POST CARDS

Ice Cream ★ Cappuccino ★ Milk Shakes

SALMON
POST CARDS

TROTWOOD PLACE

THE BOTTLENECK
Charlotte Street
Taste SOUTH AFRICAN
WINE EVERY SATURDAY
OCTOBER

Monday 18th — Friday 22nd June at 7.30pm
Broadstairs Pavilion
Tickets £8 (under 12s £4) from Festival Kiosk or...

Fish & Chips

CHIPS N FISH

34

DICKENS WALK

Nicklebys Take Awa

Childrens Menu

Dickens Cottage

Nickleby Court

Master

rnabys odge

THE CHARLES DICKENS

**RUDGE HOUSE**

**BROWNLOW HOUSE**

**DICKENS ESTATE**

Southwark Council

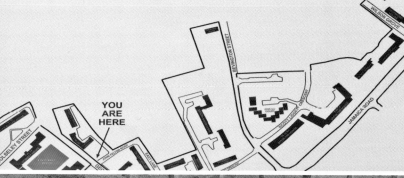

YOU ARE HERE

**CARTON HOUSE**

**DOMBEY HOUSE**

**HAVISHAM HOUSE**

**WELLER HOUSE**

**PICKWICK HOUSE**

**TUPMAN HOUSE**

**DARNAY HOUSE**

**MICAWBER HOUSE**

**OLIVER HOUSE**

# Dickens World

THE TIME OF THEIR LIVES

WELCOME

BLACKING

MANUFACTURY

PERRYBINGLE'S
PAWNBROKERS

Old Curiosity Shop

LEE BROTHERS (BOROUGH MARKET) LTD.
POTATO MERCHANTS
ESTABLISHED 1875
Also at POTATO MARKET, KING'S CROSS.

BETSEY TROTWOOD

# The Dickens Fellowship

The Dickens Fellowship was founded on 6th October 1902. Its original aims encouraged members not only to unite in friendship as lovers of Dickens's works, to assist in the preservation of buildings and objects connected with him and those works, but also to spread the love of humanity, which was the principal impulse behind his social and political thinking, and to try to remedy social evils, assisting the cause of the poor and oppressed. Contemporary aims are still much the same but also now recognise the increasing need to extend awareness of Dickens's writings to a wide audience.

Now, one hundred and seven years after its foundation, The Dickens Fellowship has a fluctuating membership of between six and seven thousand throughout the world. It has forty-eight branches, fifteen of which are in the United Kingdom, and the other thirty-three in Australia, Canada, Denmark, France, India, Japan, The Netherlands, New Zealand, and twenty in the United States. If there is no branch near to them, or if they prefer, members join the central Fellowship organisation, based in London, which has a large international membership as well as members throughout Britain.

The Fellowship and its branches organise their own programmes, which typically include talks, visits and social events. Most of them produce their own newsletters. There are annual activities like celebrations of Dickens's birth (7th February), and commemoration of his death (9th June) with a wreath-laying ceremony at his grave in Westminster Abbey. There is an Annual International Conference held in the summer. In recent years this has taken place in Amsterdam (2006), Philadelphia (2007), Durham (2008) and will be in Cleveland, Ohio in 2009. A number of these Conferences are now celebrating significant anniversaries in the life of the organising branch, either fifty years or a centenary.

The Dickens Fellowship had amongst its original membership those who would remember Dickens when alive, thirty years previously. Many of them would have been present at the public readings Dickens undertook in the last phase of his career. Immediate members of his family were involved with the Fellowship in its early years: his second daughter Katey (as Mrs Perugini), and his son Henry Fielding Dickens, were both Presidents. Later generations of the family have continued to be involved, including Dickens's descendant Monica, also a novelist, his great-grandsons Cedric and David; recently his great-great-grandson Gerald Dickens was President from 2005-7. The list of Fellowship Presidents includes, as well as family members, G K Chesterton, Sybil Thorndike, Angus Wilson, other literary figures, distinguished politicians and international academics.

The Fellowship aims to stimulate interest in Dickens and maintain awareness of his importance as the greatest English writer after Shakespeare. The sole requirement for membership has always been an enthusiasm for Dickens, his life, works, the time in which he lived. From the very beginning, emphasis was placed on this inclusive quality: it unites enthusiasts at all levels. There are scholars of international reputation in the field of Dickensian and 19th-century studies, and there are enormous numbers of general readers. There are members with interests in topography and exploration of locations, and there are those with enormous enthusiasm for amateur dramatics, reading Dickens's works aloud, and recapturing his age in costume. This means that the range of activities offered has to have a wide appeal: by doing this we enrich all of our individual experiences, and are enabled to see Dickens from many angles.

Most branches have a particular charity in which they are interested, such as the central Fellowship's 'Oliver Fund', so-called because it is always asking for more, and donates money to different charities each year, as far as possible following Dickens's own philanthropic concerns.

The central organisation of the Fellowship is based in London, at the Charles Dickens Museum, the house in which Dickens lived from 1837-9, completed *Pickwick Papers* and *Oliver Twist*, wrote *Nicholas Nickleby* and began work on *Barnaby Rudge*. It

*Above: Tony Williams, Thelma Grove & Lee Ault*

is the only one of Dickens's principal London residences to have survived and was itself almost demolished in the 1920s when the area had fallen into a decline. In 1922 the freehold became available for purchase for £1,650. The Fellowship's strenuous efforts raised the funds, the building was saved, purchased and opened to the public as a museum on the 55th anniversary of Dickens's death on Tuesday 9th June 1925.

The Fellowship publishes a journal, *The Dickensian*. Founded in 1905, it is issued three times a year and includes scholarly articles and information about Fellowship activities. Members enjoy a reduced subscription rate to the journal. In 1912, when the Fellowship was celebrating the centenary of Dickens's birth, it was able to record its pride in 'owning the only magazine of its kind, that is, one devoted entirely to Dickens.' *The Dickensian* was first published in January 1905, and was an illustrated monthly magazine, costing threepence. It included then, as now, reports of Fellowship activities ('indispensable to members as a connecting link between one and another'); original articles on Dickens's life and works 'by the acknowledged authorities of the day'; book reviews; bibliographical, biographical and topographical articles 'practically unavailable to the public today'; in fact

'everything likely to interest the student and lover of the great novelist.'

One of the heated debates with which the Fellowship began concerned its name: Society or Fellowship? The innovative nature of using 'Fellowship' to indicate 'companionship among admirers of an author' was remarked upon, and when the Fellowship came of age in 1923 there was much pleasure, both that the idea seemed to have caught on with other organisations, and that the original principles had survived.

The Fellowship is keen to make contacts with other organisations and individuals, and to give talks about Dickens, his life, works and times.

For further information, visit the Fellowship website at www.dickensfellowship.org and for the Museum at www.dickensmuseum.com or by post to
The Charles Dickens Museum, 48 Doughty Street, London WC1N 2LX.
**Dr. Tony Williams, June 2009**

# Selected Bibliography

*The England of Dickens* by Walter Dexter. Cecil Palmer 1925
*The London of Dickens* by Walter Dexter. Cecil Palmer 1930
*The Kent of Dickens* by Walter Dexter. Cecil Palmer 1924
*The Life of Charles Dickens* by John Forster. Chapman and Hall 1874
*The London of Charles Dickens* by Thelma Grove and Tony Williams 1970, 2006,
      Proof Books, The Dickens Fellowship and Transport for London
*The Making of Charles Dickens* by Christopher Hibbert. Longman Green and Co. 1967
*Dickens's England – A Travellers Companion* by Tony Lynch. Batsford 1996
*Dickens* by Peter Ackroyd. Minerva 1990
*David Perdue's Charles Dickens Page* website

# Special Thanks

Special thank you to Keith Hayley & Keith Loudon for co-financing the venture.

To James Hunt, John Cassy, Laura Green, Annalisa Johnson, Barry Taylor, George Andrew, Roger Askew, Marek Bielski, Stuart Hemphill, Jessica Balasoglou and all at SkyARTS for coming onboard as the co-producers of the programme/ film and supporting us all the way.

To Lord Hattersley, Adrian Wootton, Professor Tony Pointon, Lee Ault, Thelma Grove, Toni Mackintosh, Roger Limb, Dr Jonathan Freeman, Rev Roger Calder, Andrew Eccott and Dr. Tony Williams for contributing to the book/ TV series.

To The International Dickens Fellowship, Joan Dicks and the other council members.

To The Charles Dickens Museum, London, Dr Florian Schweizer, Kate Gazzard, Andrew Xavier.

Thank you to the following because the book, film, TV series and DVD would not have been possible without them -

Derek Jacobi, Julian Richards, Alan M Trow BSC, Simon Cox, Chris Smith, Christina Pickworth, Keith Tunney, Andrew Pavord, Karen Everett, Jeremy Fusco, Amy Roberts, Dave Ledsom, Stuart Burnicutt, Carl Proctor, Jane Burden, Wesley Burden, Suzanne Swan, Toby Eliot, Nick Coppack, Richard Juneman, Catharine Alen-Buckley, Pip Wilkinson, James Barham, Nicholas Holland, James Ingham, Daniel Elms, Ivan Palmer, Richard Clifford, Jonathan Hackett, Victoria Little, Jennifer Karen, Miriam Margolyes, The UKFC - Pete Buckingham, Alex Stolz, Kath Knight and Sara Ewin.

Dickens House Museum, Broadstairs, Mike and Gill Faulkner, Gwen Adams, June Popham, Pauline Gill, Eddie Ault; The Charles Dickens' Birthplace Museum; Portsmouth City Council; Geoff Coats; Portsmouth Historic Dockyard and Naval Pay Office; Chloe Cole; Mary Rose Trust; Chatham Historic Dockyard; Medway Council; St Luke's Church, Chelsea; St James Church, Cooling and the Churches Conservation Trust; St Giles Church, Bowes; Copnor Parish Church of St Alban; Gravesend City Council; Highgate Cemetery and Friends of Highgate Cemetery; The Old Curiosity Shop, Lincolns Inn Fields; Wightlink Ferries; Kent and East Sussex Steam Railway Line; Renault UK; Peter Thompson, Hatched Brands; Winterbourne Country House, Isle of Wight; Sean Webb & the residents of Dotheboys Hall, Bowes; Tony White and The Leather Bottle, Cobham; The George & Vulture, City of London; Barbara Hague and The Grapes, Limehouse; The Spaniards Inn, Hampstead; Coutts & Co – Jo Thorne, David Campbell and Jordan James; The Morritt Hotel, Greta Bridge; Ann Mason; Margaret Stead; 1 Lombard Street Restaurant, City of London; Garden Court Chambers, Lincolns Inn Fields; The Royal Albion Hotel, Broadstairs; Eel Pie Boatyard, Twickenham; Gordon's Wine Bar, London; Slainey Place Farm, Staplehurst; Hammersmith and Fulham Archives and Local History Centre; Highland Road Cemetery and Friends of Highland Road Cemetery; Staples Inn, Holborn; Royal Victoria and Bull Hotel, Rochester; The Chef and Brewer, Chigwell, Punch Pub Company; Waterhouse Square (Furnivals Inn), Holborn; Westminster Abbey; Kevin Christie and all at Dickens World, Chatham; St George's Hall, Liverpool; Peter Ellis; Paul Lyon Maris and Camilla Young; Triumph Interiors, London; Queens Square Fruit Stall; Port of London Authority; Livetts Launches; Abingdon Green; Emma Price; Southwark and Lewisham Film Office; The Film Office; City of Westminster; King's Bench Walk photo by kind permission of The Honourable Society of the Inner Temple; Richmond Film Office; Kensington and Chelsea Filming and Special Events Office; City of London; Camden Film Office; Covent Garden Market; Crown Estate and Paving Commission; The Dean and Chapter of Rochester Cathedral; Rochester Castle; The National Trust; Rex Features; Michael Rogers; Nick Thomas and Michelle Addison-Sakyi from Media Insurance Brokers; The staff and students of Gad's Hill School; Screen South Jo Nolan, Jenny Cooper; Film London Adrian Wootton, Jane Shaw; Key Scott Associates; Brooks Brothers UK; Liz Rees; John Sessions and Gina Fegan.

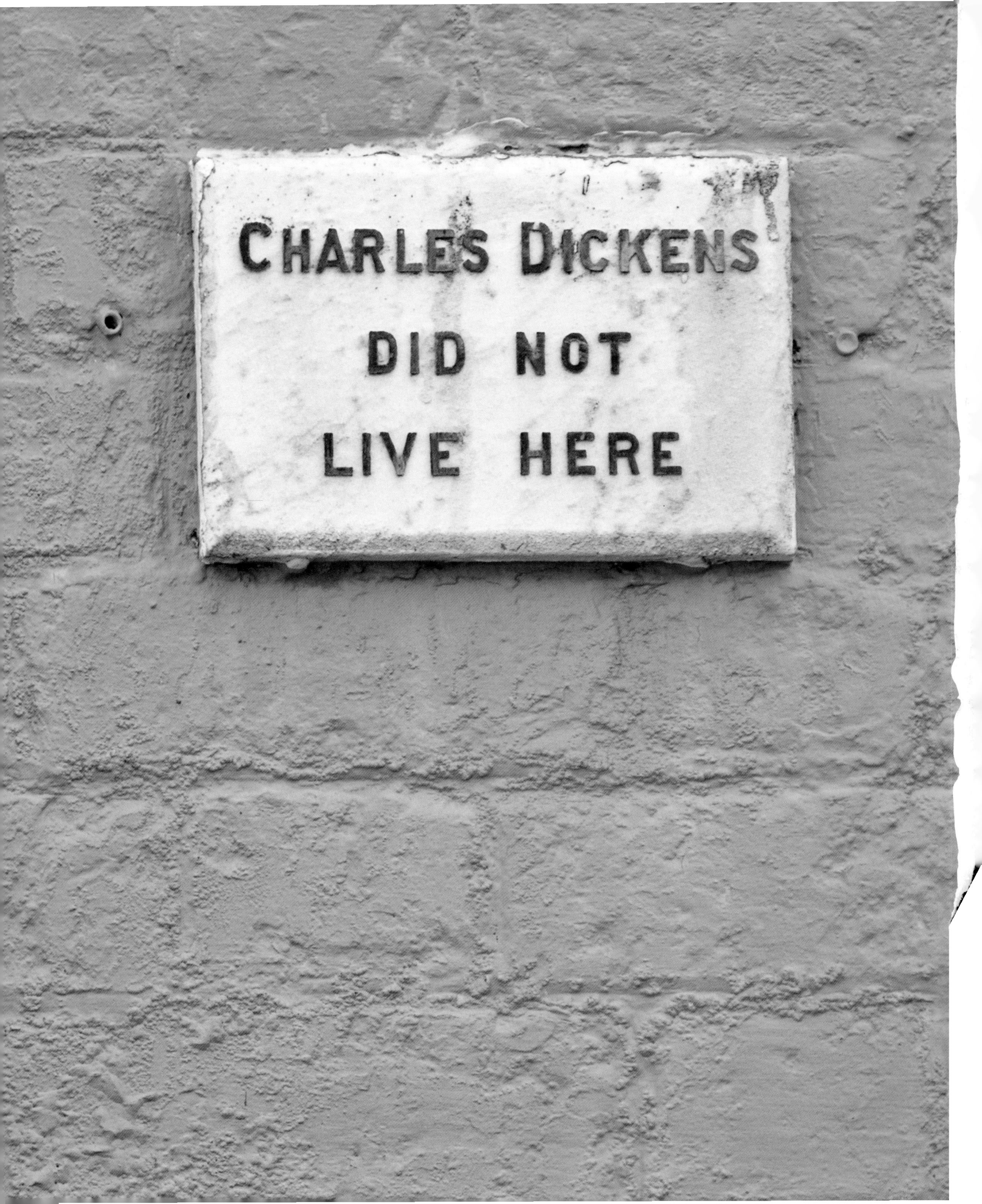
CHARLES DICKENS
DID NOT
LIVE HERE